The GPR System™

The GPR System

Charlie Wallace
Guitar Mastery Method

Copyright © 2022 - Guitar Mastery Method ® - All Rights Reserved

No part of this book may be reproduced, distributed, or stored in any form or by any means without prior written permission from Guitar Mastery Method ®.

Terms of Use

You are given a non-transferable, "personal use" license to this product. You cannot distribute it or share it with other individuals.
Also, there are no resale rights or private label rights granted when purchasing this document. It is for your own personal use only.

CREDITS | Author: Charlie Wallace | Cover design, book design & layout: Alex McLeod | Editors: Jonny Meechan, Lee Craig, Andhe Chandler & Nick Castles | Cover & live concert photography: Chris Morgan | Jam tracks: Charlie Wallace, Joshua Coyle-Te Maro & Owen Vickers | Video editor: Elmar Siriban.

www.GuitarMasteryMethod.com/GPRsystem
Register online to get online resources to go with this book.

On its release, this book reached #1 best seller status on Amazon's marketplaces in USA, Canada, UK and Australia in multiple categories.

For any inquiries, please contact support@guitarmasterymethod.com

⚠ IMPORTANT! ⚠

Register NOW for your FREE online resources & bonuses (including audio jam tracks, videos and more).

Included in your FREE bonus online resources:

- Video lessons for the 'Getting Started' module from the *10-Week Master The Fretboard Workshop*
- Access to Guitar Mastery Method's private online community
- Bonus strategy video lessons
- Audio jam tracks
- Email support
- And more...

REGISTER FREE NOW!

www.GuitarMasteryMethod.com/GPRsystem

Table of Contents

INTRODUCING THE GPR System™ — 8
- What Is The GPR System™ And Why Is It Guaranteed To Work For You? — 8
- How To Get The Most Out Of This Book — 9
- Weekly Challenges — 10
- Your Success Comes Down To This One Thing… — 11

CHAPTER #1 — 13
- How To Read A Scale Diagram — 15
- C Pentatonic Scale Pattern — 15
  - Use *"The Sprinter"* To Help Remember The C Pattern — 16
- G Pentatonic Scale Pattern — 17
  - Use The *"Mirrored G"* To Help Remember The G Pattern — 18
- D Pentatonic Scale Pattern — 19
  - Use *"The Broken Ladder"* To Help Remember The D Pattern — 20
- Why The Patterns Are Called What They Are — 21
- Linking The Patterns — 23
- Exercises To Better Remember the Scale Patterns — 24
- This Week's Practice & Challenges — 26

CHAPTER #2 — 28
- A Pentatonic Scale Pattern — 29
  - Use *"The House"* To Help Remember The A Pattern — 29
- E Pentatonic Scale Pattern — 30
  - Use *"The Lion"* To Help Remember The E Pattern — 30
- Connecting The Patterns To Link Up The Fretboard — 31
- Minor Root Notes — 33
  - Memorize The Minor Root Notes In The Pentatonic Scale Patterns — 33
- Super Memorize "The Anchor" — 36
- Super Memorize The "G+3" — 37
- This Week's Practice & Challenges — 38

CHAPTER #3 — 40
- The Difference Between Playing Scales Patterns & Actually Making MUSIC With Them — 42
- Visualize the Patterns Moving Across the Fretboard — 43
- Practice Moving the "G+3" Anchor To The Following Keys — 46
- 2 Things To Think About While You're Improvising — 46
- This Week's Practice & Challenges — 47

CHAPTER #4 — 48
- Improvising in Major and Minor — 49
- Target Notes For Major or Minor — 50
- Major & Minor Licks — 51
- The Scales Inside The Patterns — 54
- This Week's Practice & Challenges — 55

CHAPTER #5 — 56
- Memorize The Blues Scale Patterns — 56
- Visualizing The Blues Notes On The Entire Fretboard — 57
- Solo Licks Demonstrating Use Of Blues Note — 58
- How to Write A Guitar Solo — 59
- This Week's Practice & Challenges — 61

CHAPTER #6 — 62
- Diatonic Scale Patterns — 63
  - Memorize The "C" Diatonic Scale Pattern — 66
  - Memorize The "A" Diatonic Scale Pattern — 67
  - Memorize The "G" Diatonic Scale Pattern — 67
  - Memorize The "E" Diatonic Scale Pattern — 67
  - Memorize The "D" Diatonic Scale Pattern — 68
- What Scales Do I Use? — 70
- What About Theory? — 71
- The Major Scale Formula — 71
- What Notes Can I Bend? — 74
- This Week's Practice & Challenges — 75

CHAPTER #7 — 76
- What Are "The Modes"? — 76
- Memorize The Modes — 77
- This Week's Practice & Challenges — 79

CHAPTER #8 — 80
- How To Play The Modes — 80
  - The Modal Formulas — 84
- Working Out Modes — 88
  - The Modes On Paper — 89
- The Modes On Your Guitar — 91
- This Week's Practice & Challenges — 93

CHAPTER #9 — 94
- Mode Target Notes — 94

What Chords Are In A Key?	96
Moving The Modes To Different Keys	98
Using The Single Chord Backing Tracks With Different Modes	99
Mode Flavors	100
2 String Blocks	101
This Week's Practice & Challenges	102

CHAPTER #10 — 103

Simplifying The Modes	103
Playing To The Chords	104
Chord Triads	105
Finding The Taste - What Scales To Use?	107
A Visual Concept Of What You've Learned	108
Integrating Back Into Society	110
This Week's Practice & Challenges	110

BONUS CHAPTER — 112

Mixing Major & Minor Pentatonic (Aka: The 'Hybrid' Scale)	112
How To Use The Major Notes	112
Blues Scales Linked Up With Added Major Notes	113
80/20 Approach (Get started Easily By Adding Major Notes To Your G+3 Anchor)	113

Where To From Here?... — 114

IMPORTANT! READ THIS FIRST!

Dear Friend,

Your decision to grab yourself a copy of this book may turn out to be the smartest decision you've ever made to improve your guitar playing.

And it doesn't matter if you've been playing guitar for 10, 20, even 30+ years OR you're just starting out - because what you've just gifted yourself is the key to unlocking your fretboard forever.

As you are about to learn, this book completely delivers on my promise to you - You are going to finally understand exactly how the fretboard links up, know exactly how to play lead guitar in any key, and have the confidence to show your skills off in front of your friends, family, even fans!

From here on out, there's no looking back for you... Because not only have these tools given me a guitar-focused life one could only dream of, but they're continuing to give hundreds of thousands of guitar players, just like you, the freedom to play their favorite songs note-for-note, the skillset to be able to write, record, and perform their own songs, and more than anything - you are getting the confidence to whip out your guitar in any situation so you can light up a crowd at the drop of a hat.

And listen - it wasn't too long ago I found myself in a grocery store, with my hands in my pocket, rolling the loose change between my fingers... I was 7 months behind on rent payments... it was a "Do I feed me and my girlfriend, or do I feed my cats?" moment - Of course, I chose the cats because it wasn't their fault...

Guitar playing, for me, changed my life and because you, like me, are a guitar player who's wanting to dive deeper and understand this beautiful instrument further... I want to change your life. I hands-down believe THIS right here, what you now have in front of you can do that.

It works fast. It's timeless. It's your one-way ticket to fretboard freedom.

All you need to do is stay open to a very "non-traditional" approach to mastering the fretboard, put in a little work, and enjoy the ride.

I want to thank you for putting your trust in me as your guitar teacher, now let's dive in and get started!

- Charlie Wallace

Here's What Guitar Players Are Saying About The GPR System™

> Oh my f@#ing goodness!!! Another revelation moment this morning whilst traveling up and down the fretboard in any key I bloody well fancied… **Over 20 years I've been messing around…not getting anywhere, now I'm bloody Eric Clapton…** You guys know what I mean. I'm a million miles from being Eric Clapton. But I feel like him.
>
> - **Matt White**, *Kings Langley, UK*

> **It's by far the best money I've ever spent.** I've been playing, or trying to play guitar, for 3 or 4 years, spent thousands of dollars on it… wasn't getting anywhere. Then 10 Week came around… Two weeks in and my knowledge has just grown unbelievably. My confidence too especially. Best thing I've done!
>
> - **Ben Bernauer**, *New South Wales, AU*

> **I cannot believe the difference** that I can see now It's happening man. I'm finally playing and I never thought that my theory would pass. Watch out man, I'm coming. I love this thing.
>
> - **Shane Peterson**, *California, USA*

> I'm only in week 4…already totally unlocked the fretboard for me. I play from open to the 20th fret and it sounds good all the way down… **It's easier than what I had imagined…**
>
> - **Jebediah Edmonds**, *Virginia, USA*

> I've been playing guitar for over 50 years off and on, and **I learned more in the 10 week lessons than I have in almost all of those 50 years combined.** I learned more out of it than anything I've ever read or taken in the past.
>
> - **Sam Collins**, *Georgia, USA*

INTRODUCING THE GPR SYSTEM ™

What Is The GPR System™ And Why Is It Guaranteed To Work For You?

The GPR System™ stands for the "Guitar Pattern Recognition System™", and after learning this system step-by-step, you'll no longer have to think when you're playing guitar. This is because the system does the work for you by using simple, real-life imagery you already know, to create "patterns" you can recognize in an instant.

The GPR System™ allows you to focus on the important things when you play like adding emotion and being confident you're going to be playing the right notes, at the right time, every time.

To explain why The GPR System™ is so powerful... Just imagine your current guitar playing skills and knowledge as single pieces of a jigsaw puzzle... Now each piece individually has part of a picture. But when you try to put the pieces together, you find they simply don't fit...

This leads to confusion and, more than anything, frustration, because nothing you do will shed any light on how the guitar legends seem to be able to effortlessly float up and down the guitar neck like they're simply taking a stroll in the park.

The Guitar Pattern Recognition System™ builds, piece by piece, a jigsaw puzzle that fits perfectly together across your fretboard. Just take a look at this image (below), what do you see?

A house?... A sprinter?...

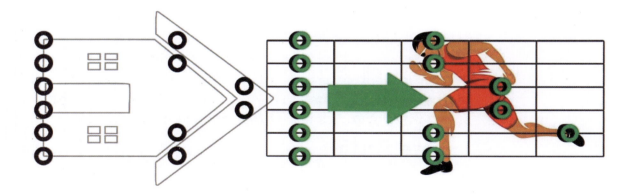

What you're ACTUALLY looking at is 2 of 5 patterns that map out your entire fretboard.

You can use The GPR System™ book (the one in your hands right now) on its own, or follow along through my 10-Week Master The Fretboard Workshop so you can visually see all the notes and patterns appear right in front of your eyes like the pros do.

And here's why I'm guaranteeing this will work for you…

Because as humans, we think in pictures, right? Allow me to demonstrate:

If I say to you - "Don't think of a RED DOOR" what can't you help but see in your brain right now? That's right, a red door. Imagine the power you'll soon possess by instantly seeing every note to play on your fretboard (and more importantly, the notes NOT to play!).

So - No more "hunt & peck" guitar solos for you, you'll have smooth transitions from the 1st fret right up to the top of the guitar neck so you can look, feel & sound like a professional with ease using the GPR System™.

How To Get The Most Out Of This Book

There's a certain mindset I like to live by when I teach you. It's actually more of a formula, and it goes like this:

The GPR System™, together with the 10-Week Master The Fretboard Workshop is my greatest training to date - And upon completion you'll understand what most consider "Advanced Theory". Pentatonic scales, blues scales & diatonic scales, to the modes Aeolian, Phrygian, Lydian, Dorian, Ionian, Locrian, Mixolydian…

And if "theory" seemed daunting before, this result-driven training will guarantee, with each page of the book (and even more powerful when combined with the available video training), you experience lightbulb moment after lightbulb moment (you know… when you suddenly "*see the light*").

But here's the thing. This training requires you to be open minded, it requires you to look through a different lens, and abandon the traditional methods used by everyone else. Here's what I mean:

You won't learn "Scales", you'll learn Scale "PATTERNS"

I'm teaching you "patterns" because "patterns" are movable. Patterns you can use more than once. Patterns are the key to learning just a few small pieces and being able to unlock your entire fretboard.

The good news for you is that there are only 5. FIVE patterns that create the foundation of every single guitar solo ever written and recorded in the history of guitar playing.

It's the bones. The skeleton of your fretboard. And you'll quickly learn this with the help of the GPR System™ book you now hold in your hands.

This book's chapters are laid out as "Weeks". The reason for this is because I want you to dedicate at least 1 week per chapter and not rush ahead. It is important that you completely absorb the information in each chapter before moving on. I'll be using both "Chapter" and "Week" to represent the 10 steps throughout this book.

It's ok if things seem a little foggy, just spend the time with the weekly challenges (more on that below) and you'll be ready to go for the next week. The danger can come when you rush ahead without the solid foundation needed to give you the skills you could only dream of before.

10 weeks are going to pass whether you do the work or not… So wouldn't you rather be the guitarist you always wanted to be in 10 weeks from now, instead of being exactly where you are right now as a guitar player?

Even if the first few weeks seem overly simplistic (which they likely will if you have ever dabbled in scales before), stick with it… The GPR System™ builds things up in a way that has never been done before in guitar training. THIS WORKS. Our members' results speak for themselves.

Weekly Challenges

The absolute most important thing is to commit yourself to this training. This is where you say *"Hell yes Charlie, I want to play killer guitar solos all across my fretboard like my favorite players"* and *"Yes, I know it is NOW OR NEVER. I am completely dedicated to mastering this"*.

Now you may want to perform for your friends and family… You may want to solo to your favorite songs alone in your lounge… You may want to become a lead guitarist and tour with your band… Whatever it is you want to achieve, I assure you, you are in the right place. This training is exactly what you need to finally understand how the fretboard links up, and how you can use it to your full advantage.

Commit yourself to the weekly challenges I'm laying out - Everyone who has experienced the true power of this training will agree. Do the challenges, it makes a world of difference!

So here's what I want you to do right now.

Grab a pen. Fill out this section below. Then post a picture of it up in the Guitar Mastery Method community!

Your Success Comes Down To This One Thing…

The results you'll see as you absorb and complete the GPR System™ Book over the next 10 weeks will be amazing but they will ONLY be amazing if one thing happens first… and if this one thing doesn't happen, then everything I've explained so far WILL NOT happen for you…

So what is it!?

Well - You need to **commit**.

I need you, right now, to make a strong decision that no matter how hard it gets at times, no matter how easy it may seem in the first few weeks, no matter how many times you feel like giving up, no matter how many times you think "I'll just do it tomorrow"…

…that you stick with me and go through these transformational lessons week-by-week.

Now I know this may sound a little crazy, but this is **VERY IMPORTANT…** You are here for a reason: There is a great guitar player inside you screaming to get out, and it is your job, and responsibility to yourself, to put in the work and make that dream a reality.

And RIGHT NOW you need to make that commitment to yourself.

Grab a pen - and fill this out, right here in this book. If you need to, grab a fresh sheet of paper and write the entire statement on the next page down, filling in the blanks with your name…

*Best time/money I've ever spent on guitar, I now know the fretboard up and down… I can grab any of the 50,000 free backing tracks on youtube and jam along, improvising anywhere along the fretboard… **I've had more "aha!" moments than I can count…** My biggest regret? That I didn't have this years ago.*

- **Tim Kerber**, *New Hampshire, USA*

YOUR COMMITMENT STATEMENT

I, _____, commit 100% to completing the GPR System™ Book & Workshop over the next 10 weeks...

By doing so, I will finally have a complete understanding of my guitar fretboard. I will be able to play, understand and use the Pentatonic, Blues and Diatonic scales, as well as the Modes so I know exactly what tools to use in any situation, to sound great. When I do this, I make my friends, family and future fans' jaws drop to the floor when I play the perfect notes in any situation.

I have waited too long in my life to be able to do what I want to on the guitar. And if I don't do it now, it will likely never happen for me.

I WANT THIS. And I declare that I, _____ will do whatever it takes to achieve complete fretboard freedom in the next 10 weeks by using the information I have in my hands right now.

Signed: _____

Date: _____

You should not move on until you have done this. Do this right now!

Each of these chapters builds from one to the next meaning you absolutely should not skip ANY of them out. Do not skip ahead in this book, your success depends on it.

You CAN go through this at your own pace and on your own schedule of course, although what I highly recommend is that you focus on completing just one chapter a week, no more.

Sound good? Have we got a deal?

CHAPTER #1

When it comes to you having complete freedom on your fretboard, this is where the journey begins. We first need to build the "Fretboard Foundation", which is much easier than it sounds.

I want you to read through this first chapter (aka "Week") to have a first run over the information. Then come back and start from the beginning again, but this time, implement each section and play these patterns on your guitar. Then finally, come back and read through everything one more time.

Each time you read through this (and I recommend you do this for each week), you'll not only get a deeper understanding of the information you have learned, but each pass through you will pick up even more information as your awareness grows.

> *"A mind, once expanded by a new idea,
> never returns to its original dimensions"*
> - **Oliver Wendell Holme**

What the above quote means, and how we can apply it to the GPR System™, is that once you learn one piece of information, your mind will become more aware of other pieces of information that it may have missed the first time.

As your awareness grows, you will soak in more information. *The GPR System™ is a MENTAL system, once you learn it in your mind, you can play it with your hands*.

Just before we dive in, it is very important that you know the difference between a scale and a scale pattern. A scale PATTERN is a series of notes that contain multiple scales inside of them. So it is VERY, VERY important that you remember you are learning PATTERNS. Once we have the PATTERNS memorized, it is very easy to play multiple scales using those patterns.

The 3 scale patterns we're covering in this chapter are the C G and D pentatonic scale patterns.

These scale shapes are based around the open chords you'll likely already know, which is why they are named the C G and D patterns (this is shown and explained in more detail later). This is the same for the other scale patterns we will use to build our fretboard foundation in the coming weeks.

Even though they are named after the chords, they are just letters to identify the PATTERNS, and the chords and scales that live inside those PATTERNS will change depending on where we move them on the fretboard.

If you're sitting there scratching your head thinking… *"Alright, this sounds weird and I don't get it"*… Don't worry, everything will become clear soon. For now, just remember the most important word here is PATTERN and not scale.

We learn scale patterns <u>first</u>, then the scales inside of them later.

These scale patterns contain multiple 'Pentatonic' scales within them.

What is a Pentatonic Scale? Stop being so nosy…

Seriously though, you don't NEED to know a lot of things that you have probably been told you do. Here's an example… Unless you paid attention in science class or you work as an electrician or rocket scientist as a profession, you likely don't know how electricity works…

But does that stop you turning on the lights at your home every night? Of course not!

You know that if you flick the switch, the light will turn on (unless the mice haven't chewed through the wiring again!).

And even if you DO understand how electricity works, you don't think about it when you flick the light switch, because why would you? The wiring has already been done, the switch is a tool that gets a certain job done… Turning on the lights.

Think of these guitar scale patterns the same way. You don't have to understand what is behind them in order for them to work.

I'd rather give you the minimal amount of information required to get the job done so you can actually experience them working with your own fingertips. Because THEN, when I explain the 'wiring', it makes so much more sense and you aren't sitting there bored while I explain wiring diagrams and how you got to get rid of the mice in your ceiling.

But since you asked… A pentatonic scale is a 'Penta' (meaning 5) 'Tonic' (meaning tone) scale. 5 notes until it reaches the same note an octave higher. An 'octave' is simply the same note higher or lower, like how you have the low E string and the high E string, both the same note, just different octaves.

Yes there are more than 5 notes in each of these scales, and that is because there are multiple scales inside these patterns, and why we learn PATTERNS instead of small 5 note scales to cover the fretboard.

If this doesn't make complete sense just yet, don't worry, just keep moving forward and come back and read this part of the book again once you've completed this first chapter.

How To Read A Scale Diagram

Scale diagrams are a small snapshot of the fretboard showing a scale pattern. In this book, fretted notes are shown as black circles, open strings are shown as white circles and the major 'Root' notes are shown in red and minor in blue.

The scale diagram (aka snapshot of your fretboard) is from the view you are looking at when your guitar is lying down flat on your lap. With the thickest string on the bottom of the diagram (in this book, the diagrams show the thickness of each string to make it easier getting started).

What is a root note? Think of it like an X marks the spot, it's a locating beacon for the scale you want to play. More on this later, for now, just remember where the root note is in each pattern.

The way you play the scale pattern on your guitar is by playing the lowest note all the way through to the highest note, and back to the lowest note.

You do this by playing from the thickest string (The low E string, called 'low' because it has the lowest pitch) through to the high E string, and back.

You'll also notice that most scale diagrams will show you what finger to use for each fret. Generally, a finger will 'belong' to one fret and play all the notes in that fret no matter what string it is on.

C Pentatonic Scale Pattern

Here is the **"C" Pentatonic Scale Pattern** in the open position.

 = Major Root Note

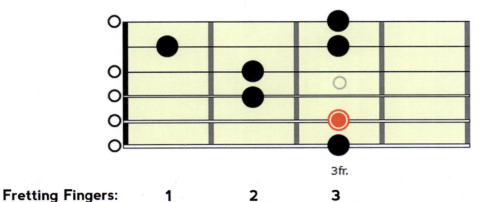

The note highlighted **Red** is the MAJOR root note for this scale "pattern". The Major root note for the C shape pattern falls on the A string under your 3rd finger.

In this position, the C pattern contains open notes, so don't forget about those!

So to play this pattern, you would:

- Play the low E string open
- Then place your 3rd finger on the 3rd fret of the low E string and play that.
- Then play the A string open,
- Then place your 3rd finger on the 3rd fret of the A string and play that.
- Play the D string open
- Then place your 2nd finger on the 2nd fret of the D string and play that
- Etc etc

So right now you can see a scale pattern on the page in front of you, but here's where the unforgettable nature of the GPR System™ comes into play….

The Guitar Pattern Recognition System™ uses imagery you've seen your entire life. It takes that imagery deeply-seated in your brain and overlays it onto your fretboard revealing an "unforgettable" scale pattern.

For the "C" shape scale pattern, in this chapter, I bring you **"The Sprinter"**.

"The Sprinter" lines up the C shape scale pattern and makes it instantly memorable.

Use "The Sprinter" To Help Remember The C Pattern

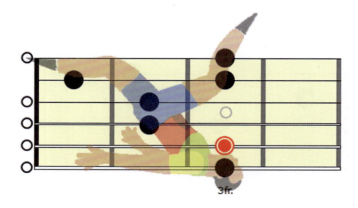

As you can see, when we flip the sprinter upside down, his body matches the notes of the scale. On your guitar fretboard, he is running the right way up, so don't worry about them being 'upside down' for now.

You can see that the 3rd fret of the low E string lands on his head, the 3rd fret of the A string on his chin, the 2nd fret of the D string on his torso, the 2nd fret of the G string on his groin, 1st fret of the B string on his calf stretching back, 3rd fret on his knee, foot back in the open position on the high e string and leading leg on the 3rd fret.

Now, when you lay your guitar down on your lap, you'll easily be able to visualize the sprinter on your own guitar fretboard. Take a look at your fretboard right now and mentally 'place' the sprinter onto your fretboard…

Now play through the scale pattern 12 times, back and forth, visualizing the sprinter at all times.

Yes, seriously do it, right now BEFORE continuing on.

Stop, grab your guitar, visualize the sprinter on your guitar and play through the pattern.

If you're wondering about how to visualize the open strings, just play them for now, we're going to be taking care of those later in this chapter (with the D pattern).

G Pentatonic Scale Pattern

The second pattern I am revealing to you is the **"G" Pentatonic Scale Pattern:**

Memorize The "G" Pentatonic Scale Pattern

 = Major Root Note

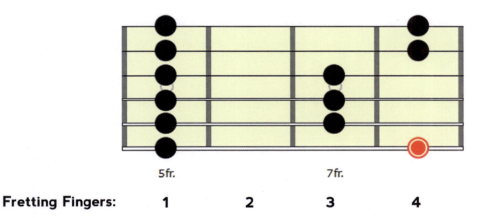

Now, we can see in **Red** that the root note for this scale pattern falls on the low E string under your 4th (pinky) finger.

Again, we just want to remember where each of the MAJOR root notes for these patterns are in the scale shape.

It'll all make more and more sense as we continue through the chapters in this book. Right now, trust in the process, and I guarantee the process will end up doing the work for you.

This pattern is built around the open G chord when played in the open position (you'll see this in a diagram in an upcoming page).

Now, this is simply a coincidence that the image used to help visualize this pattern is a "Mirrored G", you can also think of it as an "Upside-Down & Back-to-Front" 'G' as shown below:

Use The "Mirrored G" To Help Remember The G Pattern

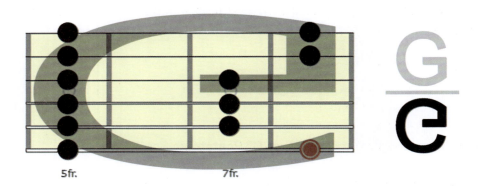

Above, we have the image overlaid on the fretboard so you can visualize how the pattern looks on your fretboard.

The G Shape Pentatonic Pattern is the guitar scale 90% of guitar players learn first. Generally played in this position too, giving it the name "A minor pentatonic scale". Forget the name "A minor pentatonic scale" if that's how you learned it.

Here's why I want you to forget that for a moment and again trust in this time-tested, proven Guitar Pattern Recognition System™...

Because when we think 'A minor pentatonic scale', we're STUCK in that one position, we can't venture outside of the box. Why we call it the G Shape Pentatonic "Pattern", is because of how it is BUILT from and so we can move this into ANY key - which I'll show you exactly how to do a little down the line, cool?

Grab your guitar, and play through the G pentatonic scale pattern 12 times back and forth visualizing the 'upside down and back-to-front G' on your fretboard.

Play through the sprinter and this G shape again before moving on. Take 2 minutes to sit and soak in those images and the notes of the patterns on your fretboard.

Then get up, take a quick break, grab a coffee, an energy drink or something a little stiffer and come back in 5 min to dive into the last pattern for this week.

D Pentatonic Scale Pattern

Now the 3rd (and final for this week) scale pattern I want to reveal to you is...

The "D" Pentatonic Scale Pattern.

And again, this pattern is built around an open chord shape (which you'll see in an upcoming diagram).

Memorize The "D" Pentatonic Scale Pattern

 = Major Root Note

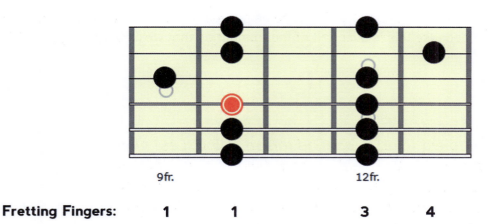

Remember the MAJOR root note shown in **Red** for this pattern is on the D string, under your first finger when playing through the scale.

For this scale pattern, we use the "Broken ladder" as a way to remember the pattern because it's pretty much straight up and down with a couple "Steps" out to the side.

Use "The Broken Ladder" To Help Remember The D Pattern

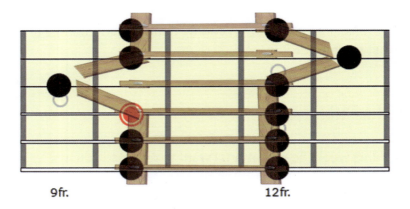

When the "Broken Ladder" imagery is placed over the top of the diagram, you can clearly identify the notes. So you only need to remember the "steps" out to the left and right of this pattern when you get down to the G and B strings.

Play through the D pattern 12 times back and forth to really lock it into your mind, overlaying the 'broken ladder' image onto your fretboard with your mind.

Once you've done that, quickly review the C and G patterns as well. These need to be cemented into your mind over this first week because this is over half of the foundation that we'll be building EVERYTHING from.

>
> *The coolest thing happened this morning. Last night I was practicing Master The Fretboard week 4. While driving my 16-year old daughter to school this morning she started talking about her ukulele practice and how it was going. She said that she was going to start to learn guitar… I asked her why and she said because she liked what I was playing last night and wants to play like me. I own two strats and I said to her that was crazy. I will let you have my SRV strat if you are serious, she said she was and she wanted to learn to play like I am playing now. So Charlie thanks to your course I now have my student to teach.* ***I wish I had this course 40 years ago.*** *Thanks so much.*
>
> **- Kevin Finch,** *Texas, USA*

Why The Patterns Are Called What They Are

Each "pattern" is named after the open chord shape it's built around. Later on, we'll actually be moving these patterns up and down the guitar neck.

Look at the upcoming diagram, you'll see the scale patterns for C G & D when they are moved to the open position on the guitar neck (this makes it easy to see the open chords inside of them). The green notes represent the open chord the scale is built around.

This isn't crucial to learn right now, but it makes things easier as we move forward with the GPR System™, and also helps explain why these are currently only "Patterns" and not actual "Scales" (just yet!).

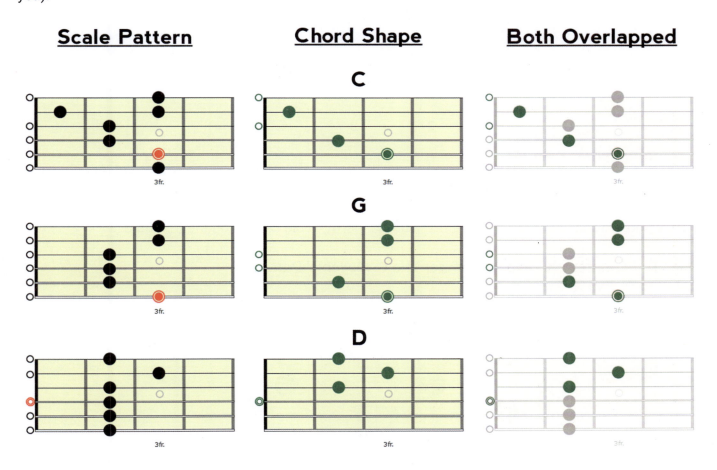

Now, remember how the "C" Shape Pattern was shown in the open position already?
Well ALL of these patterns are MOVABLE.

Like with the "G" and "D" shape, the "C" Shape also has a 'movable' pattern. If we move this pattern up to the 12th Fret we can see how the movable pattern for the "C" shape works, transforming the open notes from open position into notes you now play on your fretboard.

Movable "C" Pentatonic Scale Pattern

Note that this pattern is the same as the open position, but this time you need to fret the notes on the left side of the pattern as the strings are not "open" when played in this position.

 = Major Root Note

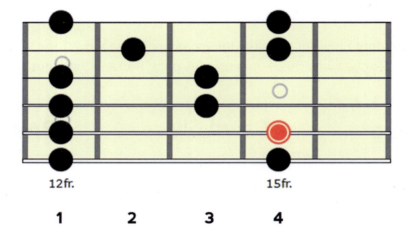

Notice the root note for this pattern in **Red** is still the same (4th) note in the scale "pattern". And these root notes stay true to the pattern regardless of where they are positioned on your fretboard.

Now, again, we can overlay the sprinter to visualize the 'movable' pattern on the fretboard.

Use "The Sprinter" To Help Remember The C 'Movable' Pattern

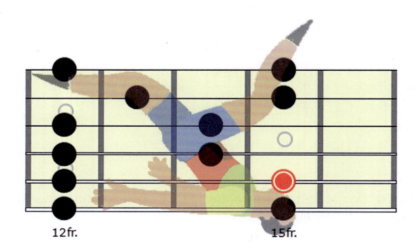

Linking The Patterns

Now that we know the 3 patterns, we can link them up to see exactly how they are positioned next to each other on the fretboard.

3 Patterns - C, G & D

NOTE: the movable "C" shape is still the same "C" shape, we just have to play the fretted notes on the 12th fret.

Pentatonic Scale Patterns Linked Up

 = Major Root Note

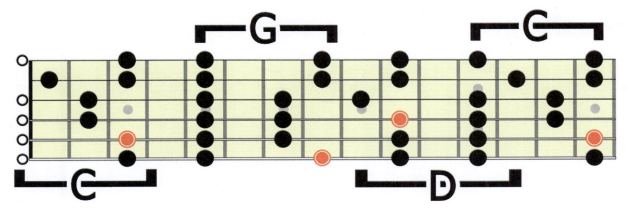

These are the patterns you've just learned, all linked up on the fretboard so you can play through them from one end to the other. Remember to pay attention to, and memorize the MAJOR root notes in **Red**.

The major root notes are ALWAYS in those positions in the scale patterns.

Now let's take a look at the patterns with the GPR Imagery overlaid:

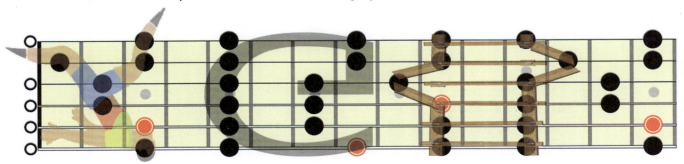

Pretty cool right? You can now play scale patterns across the entire fretboard using these 3 easy to remember images.

Exercises To Better Remember the Scale Patterns

In the optional 10-Week Master The Fretboard Workshop video course that goes along with this book, you'll see a detailed demonstration of all of the exercises. If you are just using the book alone, jump right in. And if you have never read guitar tablature before, head to the Guitar Mastery Method YouTube channel and search 'How To Read Guitar Tab' where I give you a comprehensive explanation of just how easy it is to read (it's a lot easier to read than music!).

Exercise #1 - 3-String Sets

Repeat this until you reach the high E string, then play through the pattern in reverse (aka, from the thinnest string back to the thickest string).

Example using the "G Pattern":

> Wow, just finished Week #2... **I was about to give up but after this lesson I am really jazzed** especially after playing guitar as a beginner off and on over 30 years of only knowing 4 chords and quitting over and over until now... I am totally stoked.
>
> - **Phil Lawrence,** *California, USA*

Exercise #2 - Scale Pattern in "Thirds"

Repeat this until you reach the high E, then play through the pattern in reverse.

Example using the "G Pattern":

Exercise #3 - Playing The Scale Patterns With Your EYES

Stare at your fretboard and play through the patterns WITHOUT using your fingers on the fretboard. Play the patterns with your eyes looking on the fretboard to where the scale pattern notes are. Each time you move to a new note, try to visualize the dots/notes on the fretboard just how you've seen them on the scale pattern diagrams.

Yes... I know this sounds absolutely crazy, however, this helps solidify the scale patterns in your mind VERY well. Remember, everything first comes from the mind.

This one will be slightly harder at first, however, the more you do it, the easier it is. More importantly, this will really help you develop your *"Mental Picture"* of the scale patterns on the fretboard which makes it a lot easier for you to make up great sounding solos on the spot.

Exercises #4 - Playing the Patterns With Your MIND

Whenever you don't have a guitar near you and you have a spare moment, practice playing the scales in your mind. Imagine yourself playing through each note of the pattern. Try to "Feel" the guitar in your hands.

You don't have to move your hands, in fact, it's better for this exercise to JUST use your mind.

A great time to do this is when you jump into bed and close your eyes. Visualize yourself playing the scale patterns over and over in as much detail as you possibly can. This may sound strange, but it's the most powerful of all the exercises, ESPECIALLY if performed just before you fall asleep and right when you wake up.

Every time you have a spare moment… Waiting at traffic lights, waiting in the carpark, during ad breaks on TV… Do this as much as you can. It will help your guitar playing a huge amount!

Just search NY Times for an article titled *"Olympians Use Imagery as Mental Training"* if you need more convincing on just how powerful this technique is.

This Week's Challenge

Practice *"wandering"* through the C, G and D scale patterns to a C Major Jam track. If you're using the optional 10-Week Master The Fretboard Workshop video course that goes along with this book, you can find the perfect jam tracks located in the Jam tracks section of your online members area.

On your Member's dashboard, just click TOOLS, then click JAM TRACKS and play the C Major track.

If you are just using the book alone, look up 'C Major Jam Track' on YouTube, there are a huge amount of awesome tracks in all different styles.

What is *"wandering"*? It's playing completely random notes from the scale patterns. No rhyme or reason, just play random notes. Wandering is not going up and down the scale patterns as you have practiced them before, it is purposefully playing random notes from within the pattern.

Remember, you aren't trying to make music just yet (If you are, then that's all good! But not what the exercise is for) you just want to hear how all of the notes fit perfectly to the music and get used to moving around the patterns in new ways. Plus you'll be further solidifying your complete memorization of the patterns.

I cannot tell you enough how powerful it is once you have committed these scale patterns to memory. And the best part is, it's like riding a bike, they never leave you once you have them.

Post a video into the members only community of you "Wandering" to the C Major jam track. Bonus points for the most random assortment of notes! 😉

This Week's Practice

1. Spend (a minimum) of 15 minutes every day playing through the C, G and D scale patterns and using the exercises to help memorize them. Remember to use the visual pictures of the sprinter, upside-down & back-to-front G, and the broken ladder to help remember the patterns.

2. Spend (a minimum) of 10 minutes each day "Wandering" through the scale patterns to the C Major jam track.

3. For those REALLY wanting to get great results, go through each of the exercises listed in the previous pages to lock the patterns into your mind even more.

Great work! You've made it through all the information for week #1, now it's up to you to implement it.

Remember to take your time, and soak in the information over the week to really build a strong foundation.

Next week I am going to reveal something to you that is VERY exciting, and it's already hiding under your fingertips right now…

*This was a phenomenal course! I'm 63 years old and have been playing guitar and keys for about 55 years. **I have honestly improved both my knowledge of guitar theory and my physical skill set more in the past 10 weeks than I have in the last 50 years…** Now I can jam and solo on lead guitar with confidence and I'm no longer stuck in just basic patterns. I can be creative and adjust the style to match the music pretty easily now. If you haven't taken this one (10 week MTF), I strongly recommend it!*

*- **Bob McGrath**, New York, USA*

CHAPTER #2

I hope you've been "wandering" through the scale patterns we learned in the previous chapter and practicing the 4 exercises to familiarize yourself with the 3 shapes we learned.

Those shapes were:

- The "**C**" Shape Pentatonic Scale Pattern - *Remembered by the "Sprinter" on the fretboard.*
- The "**G**" Shape Pentatonic Scale Pattern - *Remembered by the "Upside-down & Back-to-Front G".*
- The "**D**" Shape Pentatonic Scale Pattern - *Remembered by the "Broken Ladder" on the fretboard.*

In chapter #2, we'll cover:

- The remaining 2 pentatonic scale patterns, as we get one step closer to completing the "Fretboard Skeleton".
- How to find the MINOR root notes of these scale patterns.
- We're also going to learn how we can extend one of the patterns with just 3 notes to get what I've called the "G+3" (this could be the most powerful tool for your soloing and improvisation you ever learn!).

Make sure you're comfortable with Chapter #1 before moving on from this point. The GPR System™, together with the 10-Week Master The Fretboard Workshop is designed to grow with you with each chapter (or week) as your fretboard will simply link together like the greatest puzzle ever.

You don't have to be 100% certain about everything, but you should feel at least 70% - 80% confident with it, you can always come back once we link everything together to really solidify it in your mind.

So, if you're ready to continue, let's dive right in!

I have finally accomplished a goal of mine that I haven't been good enough to accomplish - until today.
I was selected as a lead guitarist for the worship team at my church... *I could not have done it without this course.*
- **Richard Drumm,** *North Carolina, USA*

A Pentatonic Scale Pattern

This is the "A" shape pentatonic scale pattern. It's built around the 'A major' open chord shape.

Notice the MAJOR root note for this pattern (in **Red**) is on the 'A' string underneath your 2nd finger.

Memorize The "A" Pentatonic Scale Pattern

 = Major Root Note

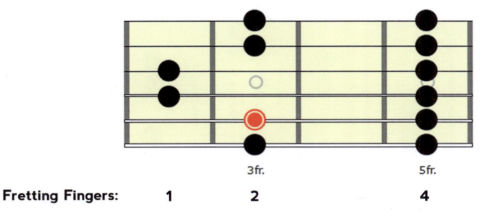

Your unforgettable GPR Imagery for the 'A shape pentatonic pattern' is "The House".

Use "The House" To Help Remember The A Pattern

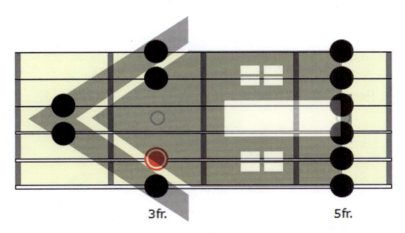

This has to be the easiest and most blatant imagery of a scale diagram on the fretboard. Play through the notes just like you did with the other scale patterns, no need for me to repeat everything here, I'm sure you've got this by now 😃.

Once you feel confident with the A pentatonic pattern, let's move on.

E Pentatonic Scale Pattern

The next pattern you need to know is the "E" Pentatonic Scale Pattern.

This is the final pattern of the 5 pentatonic scale shapes for you to learn. This one for me, when I first learned it, felt like a mashup of the C pattern and the A pattern, so make sure you pay extra special attention to the visualization on this scale to help lock it in.

Memorize The "E" Pentatonic Scale Pattern

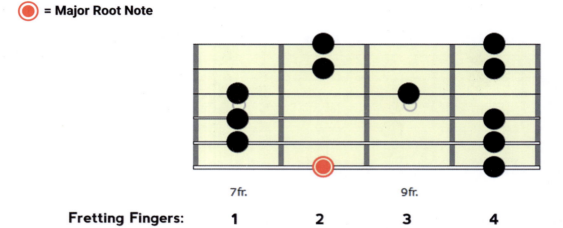

Note the MAJOR root note (in, you guessed it, **Red**) for this pattern is the Low E string under your second finger. This is also the starting note of the pattern.

And to help memorize the "E" pattern we use GPR Imagery titled "The Lion". Yes he's upside down on paper, but remember he'll be upright on your fretboard. Start on the shoulders with your middle finger.

Use "The Lion" To Help Remember The E Pattern

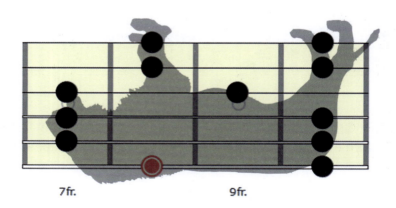

Go through both the A & E patterns until you remember them completely before moving on.

Remember, we're currently only remembering the positions of the root notes as they sit within the scale pattern - it'll all make more and more sense as we go, but this is just because we want to effortlessly 'move' the patterns, which we'll cover in the later chapters, cool? (If this made absolutely no sense to you, don't worry, we'll get deeper into it later, for now, just memorize where the Major root note is .

> *I'm on week 3 and have played for 25 years or so. Already have **learned more than I ever did from one on one lessons** at the local music shops.*
>
> - **Neil Durrett**, *Indiana, USA*

Connecting The Patterns To Link Up The Fretboard

Congratulations, you now know all 5 of the pentatonic scale patterns, and you have the mental imagery to make the foundations of your entire fretboard unforgettable!

And now that we've covered the patterns, let's look at how they link up on the fretboard so you can go from the open position all the way across your fretboard using the different shapes.

This next diagram may look overwhelming at first glance, but let's take it one step at a time and you'll see how it is really only showing the scale patterns you already know, and how they map out the entire fretboard from the 0 fret, to the 12th fret.

Look at how the brackets show each pentatonic scale pattern and see how they share notes with the patterns before, and after it. For instance, the A pentatonic scale pattern shares notes with the C pattern, and the G pattern.

You'll also notice that the patterns share the Major root notes.

Pentatonic Scale Patterns Linked Up

 = Major Root Note

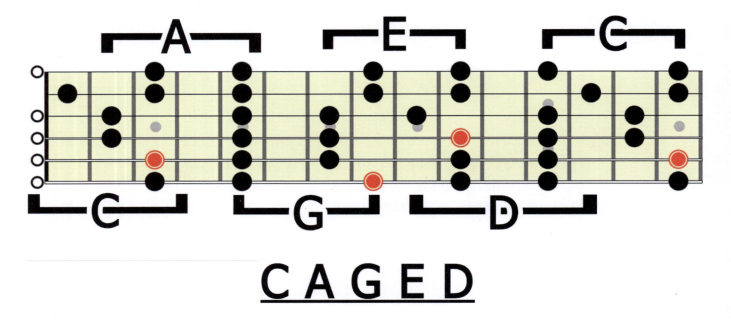

Notice how these scale patterns, when linked in the correct order, spell the word **"CAGED"**?

We can use this word to help remember how the patterns link up like a jigsaw puzzle.

You'll also see how, even without the A & E shape patterns, we still cover every note on the fretboard because the sides of each pattern complete another.

For instance, the "C" and "G" patterns play all the notes of the "A" pattern between them.

Below you can see the visualization images for just the C, G and D patterns but ALL notes from the previous diagram are included because of how the patterns overlap each other.

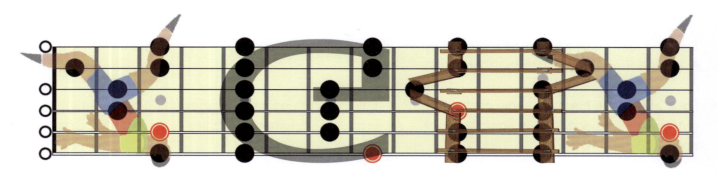

Minor Root Notes

We're going to learn the positions of the **Minor** root notes inside of the scale patterns now.

As we did with the **Major** root notes, you just want to *memorize the position* of these notes within each scale pattern because wherever the pattern is placed on the fretboard the root note position always stays the same. Take a deep breath... The memorization is almost over, trust me, it WILL be worth it. Below are all the scale patterns we've learned so far, with both **Major** and **Minor** root notes.

Memorize The Minor Root Notes In The Pentatonic Scale Patterns

 = Major Root Note

 = Minor Root Note

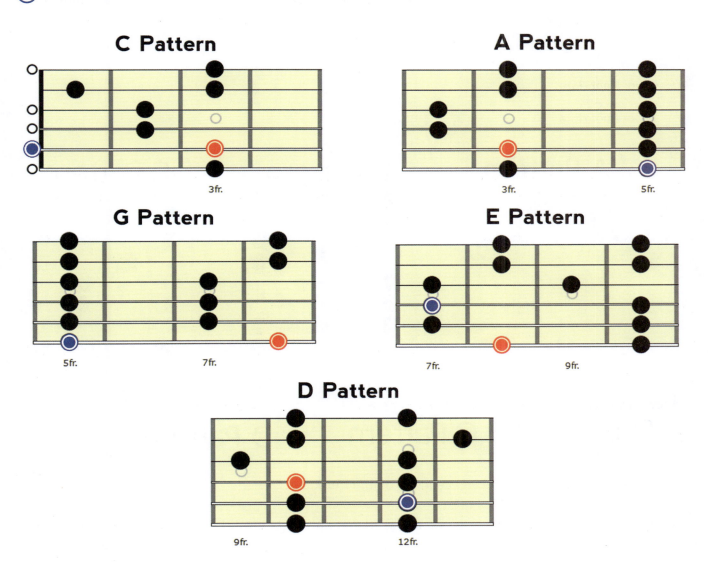

The *MOST IMPORTANT* thing you need to do right now is remember these notes within the patterns because this will allow you to play in *ANY* major or minor key and move up the fretboard through the patterns.

Remember if something feels complex, read through it a few times, finish the chapter, then go back and read through it again until you feel confident with it. A lot of what we are doing now is just memorizing where things are, so that we can put them to work later.

Trust in the process and you'll be making people's jaws drop to the floor in no time.

Notice how when the Major and Minor root note are on the same string, the Minor root note is just 3 frets down from the Major? This is a very handy thing to remember and to help you memorize where the Minor root notes are.

In the diagram below, you'll see how the scale patterns have been color coded so you can distinguish between each pattern as they're linked on the fretboard. Also included is BOTH the Major and Minor root notes.

 = **Major Root Note**

 = **Minor Root Note**

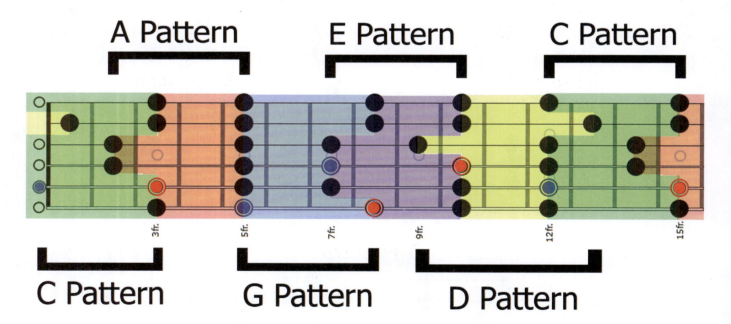

You'll notice how there are two Green sections on the fretboard.

As we move through the patterns and end the "D" shape pattern at the 12th fret, it starts the "C" pattern again then moves into the "A" shape pattern (You can see it starting at the end of the fretboard there)

These scale patterns loop around like a conveyor belt, so even if we "started" with the "G" pattern, it would still remain in order: **G E D C A G E D** So regardless of where one of the patterns is placed on the fretboard, the order is ALWAYS **CAGED**

C Pattern   A Pattern   G Pattern   E Pattern   D Pattern

Now, this may be a lot of information for you to digest and you may feel a little overwhelmed.

Good news is, you've already covered the entire fretboard and as we continue through each chapter, you'll be having more "Lightbulb Moments" where the puzzle pieces will fall into place. And very soon you'll be looking at a completely different fretboard…

In fact I bet you already are

> "What the hell Charlie?! Who said you were allowed to teach me the modes in 11 seconds??? This is ridiculous…
> **I had the names of the modes memorized within seconds thanks to the way you laid it out,** bolding and capitalizing things made a permanent visual imprint on my mind….
> What the hell Charlie?! **You're not supposed to be able to learn this stuff this fast.**
>
> **- Patrick Latour,** *Ontario, Canada*

Super Memorize "The Anchor"

Now, I want to make sure you SUPER remember this ONE pattern with the Major and Minor root notes, because we will be using this as our "Anchor" pattern (or "Home" pattern) later on.

The "G" shape pentatonic pattern. It's important you spend A LOT of time with this pattern and make it your "home base". I believe this is the most important scale pattern there is. You would have likely come across it before. Players like Hendrix, Clapton, Jimmy Page, Angus Young, Slash... They hang out A LOT in here... And with your upcoming understanding of how to move all around the fretboard, this pattern is going to become very powerful for you.

 = Major Root Note

 = Minor Root Note

G Pattern

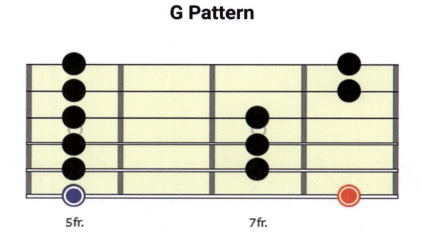

The "G" shape pattern above is currently placed in the key of A Minor because the **Minor** root note is on the 5th fret of the low E string. ('A' note)

And because the **Major** root note is placed on the 8th fret, we're also playing in the key of C Major - but we'll get to that later...

Super Memorize The "G+3"

Now we're going to add just 3 notes to the "G" Shape pattern to create the "G+3" pattern.

Using the pattern below, I want you to practice improvising in the key of A minor only using this "G+3" pattern (highlighted below in the green and yellow boxes). The extra 3 notes come from the "E" shape scale pattern.

The diagram shows the entire fretboard just so you can see where everything is, but remove all other notes from your mind and focus just on the highlighted G+3 pattern.

You'll see the 3 extra notes (9th fret on the G string, 10th fret on the B and high E strings) have created a "mini" box when you combine them with the closest notes from the G pentatonic scale pattern. Practice this box by itself to help you remember these extra 2 notes.

Improvise In Key Of A Minor Using Our "Anchor" The G+3 Pattern

 = Major Root Note

 = Minor Root Note

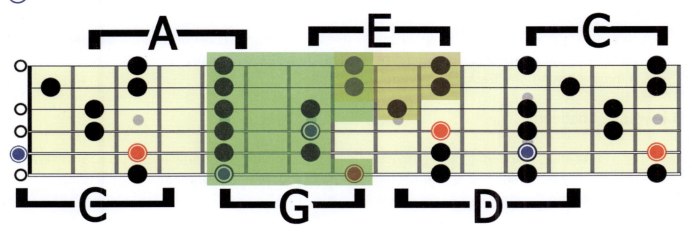

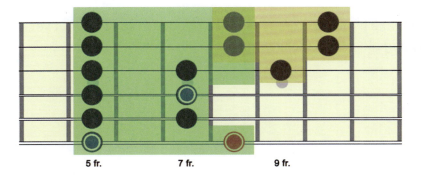

Remember, we're using these patterns to *improvise* and there's absolutely no right or wrong, you can continue to practice *"wandering"* through this pattern so you can become familiar with the added notes.

However, I challenge you to try your best to get a little more musical this week, try putting some notes together that sound good, try creating a few licks, or maybe use some licks from solos you have learned that fit inside of the scale patterns?

Next week, we're going to be getting into a bit of a solo 😀

This Week's Practice

1. Use the exercises shown in Chapter #1 to memorize the A & E patterns (check back to the previous chapter for a reminder on these exercises).

2. Memorize the **Minor** root notes inside all 5 Patterns.

3. Go over how the patterns link up over the fretboard **EVERY DAY** both by looking at this material and playing the patterns on your guitar, really focus on how they link up.

4. *"Wander"* around the whole fretboard moving between the patterns in both your mind and with your fingers.

5. Use the "G+3" anchor to start improvising in the key of A minor. Use the A minor jam track you will find in your members area. (click on "Tools" then "Jam Tracks") or any A minor backing/jam track you can find on YouTube.

This Week's Challenge

Record yourself either *"Wandering"* or improvising using the pentatonic patterns linked up over the entire fretboard in the key of A minor, using the A minor jam track you have in your members' area or on YouTube.

You must play notes from **EVERY** pattern (hold yourself to this rule… It's important and worth it!)

Remember, if you can make it musical, great! If you're not quite ready for that yet, just *"wander"* for now. We will add more building blocks for making *"music"* next week!

A Favor To Ask You, But Not For Me...

People who help others (with no expectation) experience much more fulfillment, live longer and enjoy life 10X more than the average Joe. I'd like to give you the opportunity to deliver this value to you during your Guitar Mastery Method experience. In order to do so, I have a simple question for you...

Would you help another guitar player you've never met, if it didn't cost you a single cent, but you never got any credit for it?

If so, I have a small 'ask' to make on behalf of someone you don't know. And maybe you never will...

They are just like you, or like you were when you first picked up a guitar: less experienced, filled with the desire to play, potentially wanting to perform and impress their friends & family, and seeking the right information but they've got no idea where to look... This is where you come in.

The only way for us at Guitar Mastery Method to accomplish our mission of helping the world's guitar players is by first reaching them. And you have to agree, most people judge guitar lessons solely based on their reviews. So... If you have found these lessons valuable so far, would you please take a brief moment right now and leave an honest review of this book and its contents? It'll cost you zero dollars and take less than 60 seconds.

Your review will help...

...one more guitar player to finally understand their fretboard
...another guitar player to cut days, weeks, even years of practice
...another guitar player find happiness in what they're playing instead of all that frustration
...one more guitar player's life change for the better

To make that happen, all you have to do is (and this takes less than 60 seconds)... leave a review.

Here's how:

Go to the book page on Amazon and leave a review right there on the page. Just search "GPR System" or "Guitar Mastery Method" and it will come up.

If you're feeling good about doing this for a struggling guitarist you'll probably never meet, then you are an amazing human yourself and we welcome you into the Guitar Mastery Method world with open arms!

Thank you for helping us help more guitar players around the world.

CHAPTER #3

We've covered quite a lot of knowledge in the previous chapters, getting all 5 pentatonic patterns memorized using the imagery, plus linking them up on your fretboard.

Now we're going to start using this knowledge and multiplying it to use in different ways. First of all, we're going to learn a simple guitar solo in the key of 'Am' using the 5 scale patterns

You can find the backing track for this in your members area. Refer back to the start of this book to get your online access.

This backing track is a simple 12-bar-blues that we're going to be playing over, and you're simply walking through the patterns you already know. It's a very simple solo, and this is because I want it to be as easy as possible for you when you first move this solo into different keys.

The guitar tab for the solo is on the following page. If you'd like extra help in exactly what fingers to use, I cover that in the optional 10-Week Master The Fretboard video course.

First focus on getting the notes and techniques down, then start practicing with the backing track.

You'll notice for this solo we've used all 5 of the pentatonic scale patterns. We started with the "A" pattern, moved up into the "G" Pattern, then slid up on the higher strings to the "E" pattern, into the D pattern, then back down into the C pattern to finish off the solo.

Remember, the track is inside your members area.

One thing to remember with the blues is that we play **minor lead over major backing**, so even though this doesn't say "A minor", we still play in minor because it is a blues track.

We'll dive into the 'WHY' behind that soon 😉

The Difference Between Playing Scales Patterns & Actually Making MUSIC With Them

If you've ever felt as if you're *"stuck in the boxes"* or you're struggling to make music when you play… It's simply because you've learned the patterns in such a logical way that they may not actually sound as musical as you'd like them to when you play through them…

However, if we take the intro to Jimmy Page's solo in Stairway to Heaven… This solo begins using the G+3 pattern with a whole bunch of licks, but you're not going to tell me that Jimmy Page is *"stuck in a box"* are you? It's one of the greatest solos of all time, right?

Right now, it's easy to become oblivious to the result because at the moment, what you've done is all very logical, and in more of a 'scientific' way you've learned it all.

So don't worry if it's not so musical for you just yet because you're going to be getting a lot more "artistic" as we continue. Keep on jamming with these scales and improvising your own style, and please don't underestimate the power of the tools you've already learned!

When I was a youngster working at my local music store called Music Machine, a local legend in the blues scene walked in one day, and could see me behind the counter going through these same scale patterns you are learning now. He took his eyes away from the new line of Fenders that had just arrived and came over to the counter. He said… *"You know, every weekend when I'm not playing a show, my friends come over. We have some drinks in my garage and I get up some backing tracks on my computer and crank them through the stereo. Then I crank my guitar up and start soloing. They all think I'm Hendrix or Clapton, but really, all I'm doing is just playing in the scale patterns you're doing now"*.

I already knew this to be true, but hearing someone else reveal "the secret" made me wonder why it had to be a "secret" all along? But hey… That's why this book exists 😃

Visualize the Patterns Moving Across the Fretboard

"Where the ROOT NOTES are positioned on the fretboard determine what key the patterns are placed in."

After all this emphasis on learning root notes, you will now see why they are so important.

In music there are only 12 notes. You have 12 positions to put these scale patterns in to get ALL Major and Minor keys. And you know we've been practicing the patterns in the key of C Major and A Minor, so you only have 11 more positions to learn…And don't worry, you're about to get this part so damn quick you almost wouldn't believe it.

Just before I reveal the next GPR System™ secret to you, it's crucial that you fully understand how the scale patterns link up, and have memorized the positioning of the root notes inside of the patterns. If you don't have this 100% dialed in, revise over the previous chapters and meet me back here when you're good to go. It WILL be worth it.

Here are the 5 pentatonic scale patterns linked up in the key of C Major and A Minor.

◯ = Major Root Note

◯ = minor Root Note

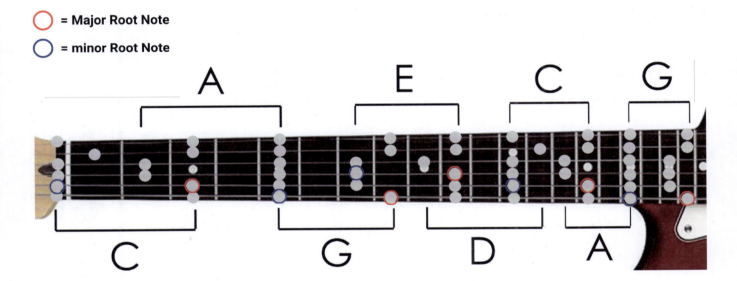

The **Red** notes (AKA Major Root Notes) and the **Blue** notes (AKA Minor Root Notes) dictate what key we're playing in. So at the moment all the **Red** notes are sitting on "C" notes and all the **Blue** notes are sitting on the "A" notes.

Now here's where you take everything you've just learned to the next level, metaphorically AND literally!

Let's move everything up **one fret**. Now the **Major** root notes of the pattern are sitting on "C#" and "Db" (remember, that is the same note, just two different names) which is positioning the patterns into THAT key, and of course it has its relative minor (A#/Bb).

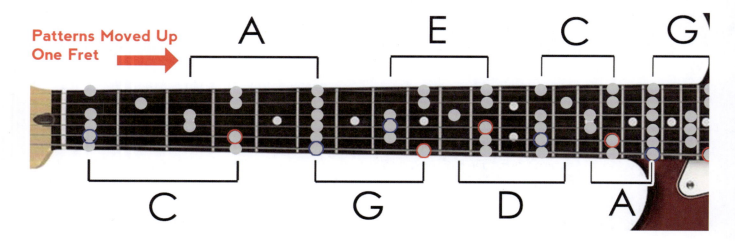

As we move up another fret, you can see the patterns stay exactly the same, it's just that everything has moved up - moving it to another key. We call this "The Fretboard Conveyorbelt".

You can see here that the "D" pattern, which links up to the end of the "C" shape is starting to creep in on the left hand side (at the beginning of the fretboard). And as you know, the patterns spell the word 'CAGED', infinitely repeating - C A G E D C A G E D C A G E D.

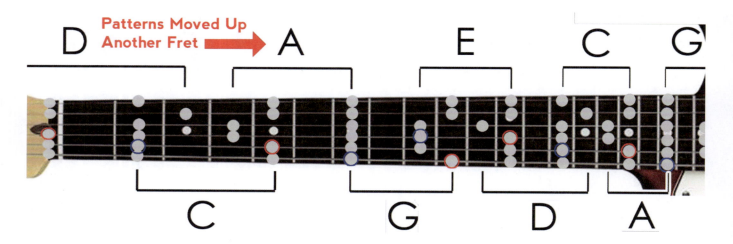

We've moved up another fret and another key (shown above) so we're now in B Minor, with the relative minor, D Major.

I recommend, right now, you take a breath... This can be A LOT to take in, and it's one of those "No way... That's too easy" kind of things. Do not overthink this, it's just like trying to look for the mountains in the distance when something is right in front of your face... Very easy to miss. Go back 2 pages and read through this again. The last 2 pages have just dropped a BOMBSHELL which is going to unlock so much for your guitar playing. Go back now... Go! 2 pages!!

Here's where you finally understand how you can play in any key, because all you have to do is take the "G+3 pattern" (homebase/our "Anchor") and position the Major or Minor root note of the note of the key you want to play in.

From there, all the other scale patterns link up with the G+3 pattern, which links up the entire fretboard.

And we don't JUST have to use the G+3 to position ourselves into different keys (although, it's a pretty damn good idea, I still do this EVERY SINGLE TIME… But it is good to at least know other ways to help understand how it works). For example, if you wanted to play in the key of F Major and chose to use the "C" Pentatonic scale pattern, all you have to do is position the Major root note of that scale pattern onto an F note… Done! All the rest of the patterns get in line and you have every single note you can play in the Pentatonic scale in the key of F Major over the entire fretboard.

Here's An Example (In the key of F Major):

◯ = Major Root Note - F

◯ = Minor Root Note - D

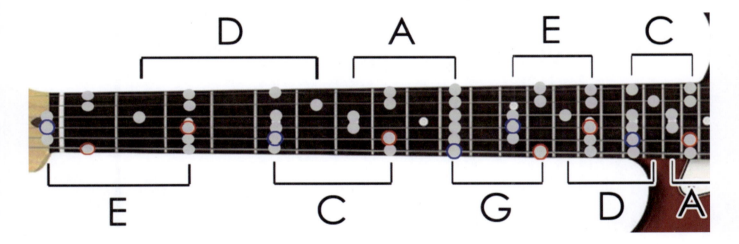

This IS The Secret

If you have memorized all 5 of the pentatonic scale patterns, memorized the major and minor root notes in each of them PLUS understand how to move those patterns up and down the fretboard into different keys… Even if you're still letting it digest… You now know more than 99% of guitar players in the world.

The best part is that from here on in, we are only going to be adding to the knowledge you have already built. The ultimate foundation has been laid, so don't worry if this all feels like trying to drink from a fire hose.

Practice Moving the "G+3" Anchor To The Following Keys

Move the **Major** and **Minor** root notes of the G+3 pattern to the different keys written below. This is a great exercise to really lock in this concept.

We're not changing the pattern we're playing, we're just changing **WHERE** we play the pattern on the fretboard.

Remember the Minor root note in the G+3 pattern is your index finger, and the Major root note is your pinky finger:

A Minor	**Db Major**
D Major	**F Major**
C# Minor	**F# Minor**
Bb Minor	**Eb Minor**
B Major	**G Minor**
C Major	**A Major**
D Minor	**B Minor**
G# Minor	**E Minor**
C Minor	**F Minor**
F# Major	**Ab Major**

2 Things To Think About While You're Improvising

I'm just about to give you this week's practice… But before I do, I wanted to give you a couple of things to think about when you're improvising this week:

1. Timing is important. You now know which notes to play to be in key. Now work on hitting those notes in time to the backing track you are improvising over. You can ALWAYS go back to the BEAT of the song if you feel you have fallen out of time. This will become "instinctual" in time and won't always be something you consciously have to focus on.

2. Repeating notes makes things easier and sounds more musical. This can be single notes or groups of 2, 3, 4 notes, or more (think of the Stairway To Heaven solo, a few times Jimmy grabs onto a short lick and repeats, repeats, repeats).

This Week's Practice

1. Learn the "Solo in A minor" and play this solo over the "A Straight Rhythm" blues jam track on the "Blues Jam Tracks" page inside your members area.

   Note: even though this jam track doesn't say minor, we still play minor over this. As with blues music, we play minor solos over major jam tracks to get a bluesy sound.

2. Continue improvising, focusing on the 2 things to think about mentioned on the previous pages (timing and repetition).

3. Practice moving the G+3 Anchor to different keys (Use the Chart shown above and "wander" around the notes).

4. Once you're comfortable moving the G+3 anchor to different keys, begin wandering throughout all of the patterns over the entire fretboard in different keys (remember, if you get lost, jump straight back to the G+3 Anchor).

This Week's Challenge

Transpose the guitar solo you learned in the key of A minor into the key of D minor. Record a video of you playing the guitar solo in the key of D minor to the "D Jivey Shuffle" jam track on the "Blues Jam Tracks" page inside your members area.

You might be asking yourself... **What on Earth does "Transpose" mean!?** It just means "change the song/solo to a different key".

IMPORTANT note for this week's challenge...

This is your toughest challenge yet. Not only are you thrown in the deep end with no reference material in the key of D minor, but the jam track you're going to be playing the solo to is quite fast. This is a CHALLENGE and NOT meant to be easy. This is meant to stretch your abilities. Chances are you are going to feel frustrated, but stay with it. Spend 30 Minutes a day working on this challenge and upload a video showing how far you get.

Remember this... You don't have to get it perfect, you just have to get it started, because this will set you up for the coming weeks, making it much easier down the line.

Even if, in your video, you can't keep up with the jam track, you're hitting the wrong notes and you're falling on the floor... upload it anyway! It's important to keep up with the challenges and upload your videos! 😊

CHAPTER #4

We're almost halfway and we're really making progress. Do you already feel like a whole new world has opened up for you on your fretboard? If you're like most of my students who have gone through the GPR System™, at this point, you might feel like you finally understand what you once thought was impossible…

And the best part? Everything from here on in is just going to add onto what you have already learned so far.

You've covered a lot of ground… From the 5 patterns with the **Major** and **Minor** root notes, to understanding how to improvise through all of the different keys using the G+3 pattern.

We've almost completed the "Skeleton" of the fretboard and as we progress, we're going to start adding in extra notes and building upon what you've got so far.

In this chapter, we're looking at the scales inside of the patterns you've learned. I want you to review this chapter multiple times to make sure it really sinks in.

Improvising in Major and Minor

In the 10-Week Master The Fretboard Workshop we've been jamming in the key of A minor and we have been playing minor over major to get that bluesy sound. This ONLY works with blues music, however we can also play Major. If it's blues in "A" for example we can decide what kind of sound we want.

Now, try not to get this confused with "Blending Major and Minor", that is a different thing (which we will get to). For this exercise, I want you to only play either Major or Minor using the G shape pattern and position the Major or Minor root note for the G pattern on the "A" note

>
> *I just started week #3 of mastering the fretboard. I think my mind is going to pop… I've been trying to learn guitar for a year and a half & I've learned more in two weeks than I've learned in over a year ! **This is Amazing** Charlie Wallace you are my new hero.*
>
> **- Kurt Moore,** *Oklahoma, USA*

Improvising In A Major & Minor Using The G Pattern

🔴 = Major Root Note   **Red** notes showing G pattern in "A Major".

🔵 = Minor Root Note   **Blue** notes showing G pattern in "A minor".

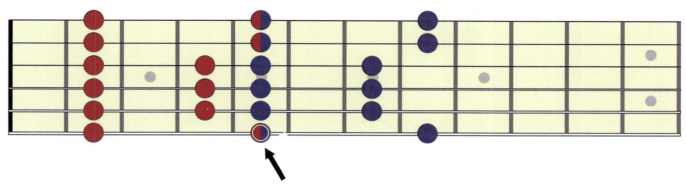

Use the 5th fret to position the G Pentatonic scale pattern in both A Major and A Minor by using either the major or minor root note in the pattern.

Notice that we're using the G shape pattern, and starting on the "A" note but we either use our pinky starting on this note for the Major sound, or our index for the Minor sound.

The **Red** notes are showing the pattern in the key of A **Major** in the diagram above. And the **Blue** notes are showing the pattern in the key of A **Minor**.

When playing the Major scale over the track, you want to make sure to target the Major root notes. You don't have to start on these root notes, but this will make it sound more natural.

You can then play any random assortment of notes in the scale pattern making sure you target (aka hold onto) the root notes. Plus ENDING on a root note is always a good idea and makes sure you sound like you know EXACTLY what you're doing.

For instance, you could start on the low E string on the 5th fret, then play some of the other notes in any random order a bit faster, then hold onto the next root note (2nd fret on the G string in this particular key), then go back up and down the scale pattern quicker, ending on a big long hold on the 5th fret high E string, which is where the highest root note in this pattern is located.

Target Notes For Major or Minor

Red target notes for Major

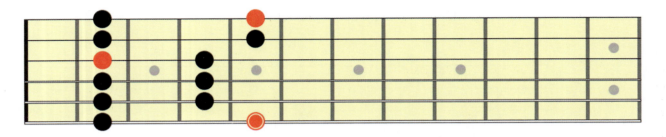

When we move the pattern up into the key of A minor, we can see the **Blue** target notes for this scale, again, you don't have to start on these notes and you can play any random assortment of notes, just make sure you make a point of targeting these root notes to keep the solo sounding right!

Blue target notes for Minor

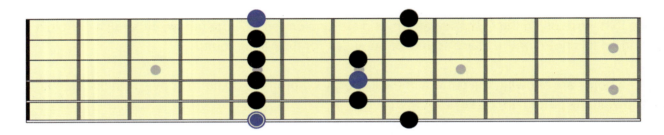

Soloing in Both Major and Minor to Jam Tracks

Inside your members area, jam to the "A Straight Rhythm" jam track.

Remember, that with blues we can solo in both major or minor UNLESS it states that it is a "Minor Blues" in which case you can only solo in minor.

Practice focusing on the different "target notes" for both major and minor using the G pattern.

On the next page are some examples of Major and Minor licks you can use over the backing track.

Major & Minor Licks

Major Lick #1

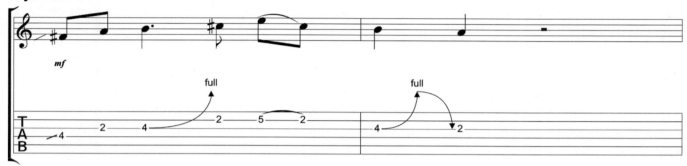

Major Lick #2

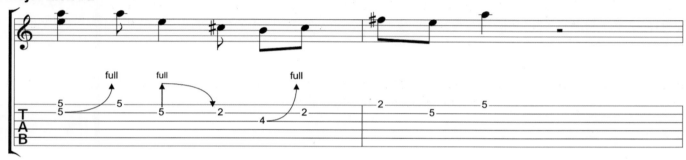

minor Lick #1

minor Lick #2

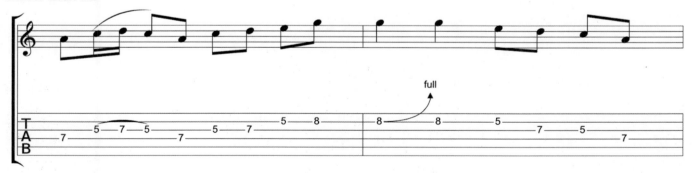

These licks will give you a great place to start as you improvise your way through the backing track switching between the major and minor scale.

Remember to use the diagrams on the previous page if you get lost on which scale to use, and which target notes to hit.

You've also learned some tips in the previous week to help you with improvising. If you're still having trouble making it sound musical, head back to the last chapter and check out the pointers there.

Here's another exercise that's going to help you with finding the root notes (both major and minor) inside of all 5 pentatonic scale patterns.

I want you to go through these patterns and find the other root notes for each scale. Remember, you already know how to name all of the notes on the fretboard using the octave trick, so that's a head start 😊.

Just grab a pencil and get into it, you can just circle them in the book and when you're sure of the notes, if they're major or minor, use a blue and red pen to confirm they are **Major** or **Minor.**

Circle the "Target Notes" for both major and minor keys
(use a different colored pen for major and minor)

 = Major Root Note

 = Minor Root Note

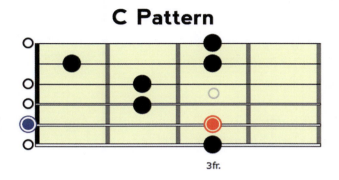

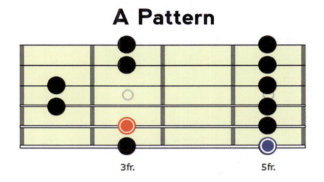

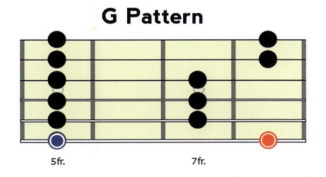

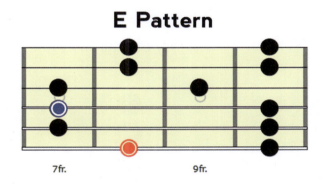

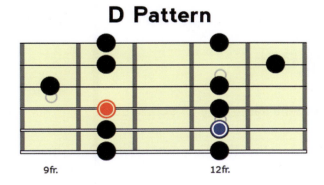

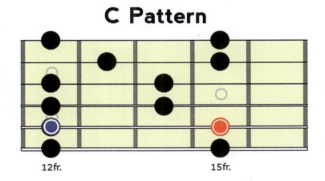

The Scales Inside The Patterns

Remember how we're playing "Scale Patterns"? The scales themselves are inside of those patterns, and are very easy to play.

To play a **Major** Pentatonic Scale, we simply begin on the Major root note of any of the Pentatonic Scale Patterns, then play through the pattern until we reach the same note, an octave higher. To play a **Minor** Pentatonic Scale, we do the exact same, but start on a Minor root note.

The patterns do all of the hard work for us, it doesn't matter what pattern you use, as long as you start on a root note. And when we cover the diatonic scale patterns later in this book, the exact same principle applies to playing diatonic scales.

With Pentatonic scales having 5 notes, we are only playing through 'part' of the scale pattern. And for the scale to sound 'complete' we actually play 1 more note as we are repeating the first note we played an octave higher.

Here's an example... To play a C Major Pentatonic Scale, we position any Pentatonic Scale Pattern (in this diagram, showing the G Pentatonic Scale Pattern) with the Major root note landing on a C note.

Play from this note (the Major root note of the scale pattern)...

...Through the scale pattern until you get to the same note an octave up.

Because we know the Major and Minor root notes, and we know that there are 5 notes in a Pentatonic scale, we can simply grab any root note, play through 5 notes from the root note, then just 1 more note (which is repeating the first note you played an octave higher) and you just played a Pentatonic scale.

Take some time now, and play through **Major** & **Minor** Pentatonic scales inside each of the 5 Pentatonic Scale Patterns you know.

This Week's Practice

1. Solo to the A Straight rhythm jam track using both Major and minor scales as described on the previous pages.

2. Practice playing both major and minor scales inside the pentatonic scale patterns.

3. Learn the major and minor solo licks on the previous pages to add into your improvisation.

4. Improvise playing in as many keys as possible. Search for jam tracks to use on YouTube for an unlimited variety of keys and styles.

5. Complete the diagram on the previous page by circling the Major and Minor root notes within the scale patterns to find the target/root notes for each pentatonic scale pattern.

6. Have a recap over all of the previous chapters. We have now built the 'Skeleton" and going forward we will be adding to this to create different types of scales.

This Week's Challenge

PART 1: Record yourself improvising to the C Major jam track focusing on the MAJOR target notes. Jam track is found in your GPR System™ members area.

PART 2: Record yourself improvising to the B Minor jam track, focusing on the MINOR target notes. Jam track is found in your members area.

That's all for this week!

> *Wow, I have just started week 3 Master The Fretboard and it just clicked, **I now have the knowledge to solo in any key minor or major anywhere on the fretboard.** Master The Fretboard is by far the best investment in my guitar playing I have ever made.*
>
> - **Tony Urey-Guest**, *Shropshire, GB*

CHAPTER #5

Quick check in before we dive in: You NEED to have been through the previous chapters for any of this to make sense to you. **Remember, each chapter builds upon one another**. Now, in this chapter, we're going to add an extra note into your scale patterns to make the "Blues Scale". This one note makes a huge difference in the sound. The blues notes are shown as hollow, light blue circles on the below diagrams. These are using the EXACT pentatonic scale patterns you already know, just adding an extra note. The patterns in the following diagrams are positioned in the key of C Major & A Minor.

Memorize The Blues Scale Patterns

 = Major Root Note    = Blues Note

 = Minor Root Note

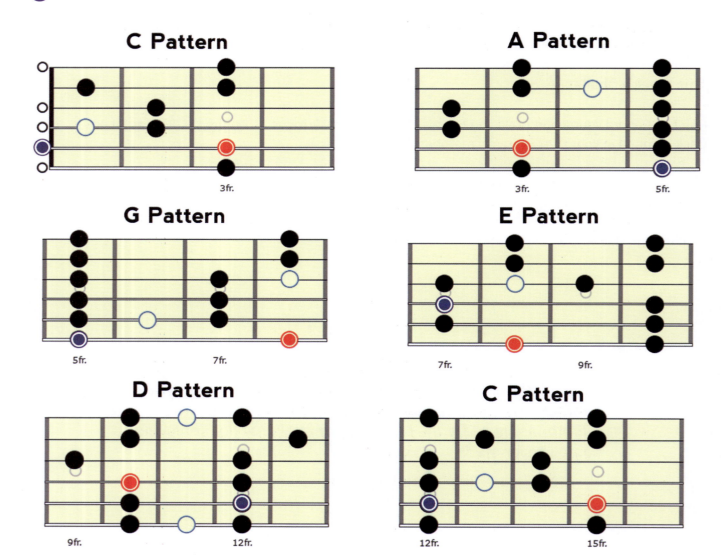

Remember there are only 5 patterns and we're just adding one note into the pattern. The note is the same in every pattern and in some cases appears twice within the scale pattern. For example, we can see that in the D pattern, the blues note is on the low and high "E" string.

I've also put the C pattern here twice, once in the open position and once with the movable pattern at the 12th fret.

Pick two of the scale patterns and practice them each day, adding in the blues notes as you play through them, really focus on two scales per day to help them get locked into your mind. At this point, it may feel like we're rushing through here... Stick with me, and take your time to memorize where to add these blues notes. It is really as simple as that. I don't expect you to memorize them all right now, take the week, let them soak into your hands & mind.

Visualizing The Blues Notes On The Entire Fretboard

Below is a diagram of the entire fretboard showing the "Blues note" for the key of C Major/A Minor. This is adding into the "skeleton" we've just completed building over the last 4 chapters. Each pattern is shown in a different color so you can easily see how they "jigsaw piece" into each other.

 = Major Root Note    = Blues Note

 = Minor Root Note

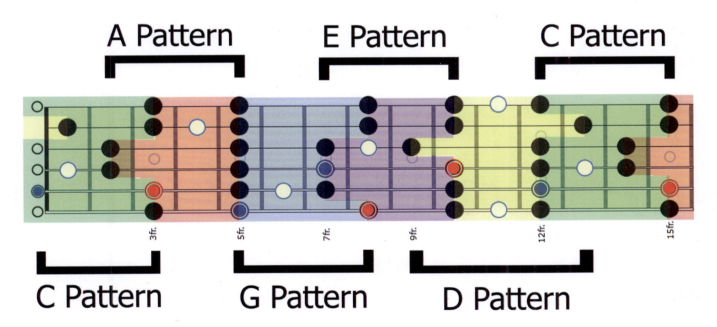

The "Blues Note" is a passing tone to give you the bluesy sound, we don't 'hang' on this note. A great way to think of it is building tension and releasing into a resolving note for the key you're playing in. The licks below will help you hear this (blues notes circled in blue to make it easy).

Solo Licks Demonstrating The Use Of The Blues Note

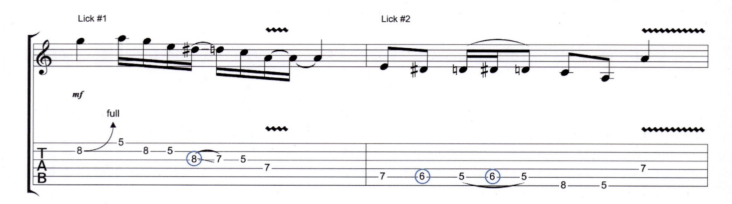

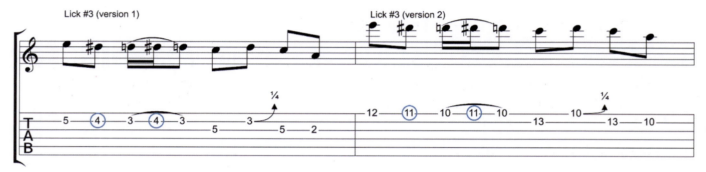

Now you know how to apply the blues note to your soloing and improvising. So go back to all the jam tracks you've played around with so far and start experimenting.

Getting used to these blues notes comes with exactly that… Experimentation.

You already know the patterns and you're just adding one note in, walking into it, sliding over it, bending into it. You'll get used to it real quick.

Memorize those blues notes and your improvisation will instantly start sounding more "bluesy".

How to Write A Guitar Solo

By now, you have already been writing guitar solos, whether you know it or not. You have been doing this with your "improvisations". Every time you improvise, you are literally writing a guitar solo. It really is that simple.

For me, when I go to write a guitar solo for a song, I play the track over and over again, looping over the part I'm going to be soloing over. I get the scale patterns in the right key and start playing around, trying to get a "feel" for things.

Then I start out by trying to find something that sounds good to start on. Maybe it's a big high bend to a root note, maybe it's sliding into a lower root note, maybe it's coming straight out of the gate like a raging bull throwing notes all over the fretboard…

Every song will ask different things of you as a guitar player, and as you develop your skills, and listen to what the song is wanting, you'll start to understand just how these great guitarists write amazing guitar solos.

There is no "right" or "wrong" way to write a guitar solo. There are an infinite number of ways to approach writing a solo, but my favorite is simply improvising over and over until I play the exact same thing (or close enough) every time.

I do this by finding areas in the solo. Once I have something that works in the beginning of the solo, I'll try to find the next part, but I'll just keep going until the end of the solo, improvising the whole way.

I might not find the beginning straight away, or the part that follows that, however I might find a cool lick I want to use in the middle of a solo, or closer to the end.

If you have the optional 10-Week Mastery The Fretboard Workshop, have a watch as I explain this topic in depth.

Here are some points to remember:

- Replay the backing music over and over and over and over
- Go from the start and improvise a few times
- Once you have something you like for the first bit, play that every time you start
- Keep adding piece by piece until you have a finished solo you're happy with
- Take a look at how some of your favorite guitar solos are structured, where do they start, how do they end?

When I was recording with legendary producer Michael Wagener who has sold over 100 Million records with bands like Metallica, Ozzy Osbourne, Mötley Crüe, Skid Row, Alice Cooper & more… He said a great way to "tell a story" with a guitar solo is to start low and slow, end fast and high.

"Start low and slow, end fast and high."
- **Michael Wagener**

Think about one of the greatest solos of all time, Stairway To Heaven, that's a great example of this.

Of course not every solo has to start low and slow, just listen to what the song wants. Sweet Child O' Mine starts with a higher note than what it ends on, but Slash takes it slow and is very melodic in the beginning, repeating the same rhythmic motif over and over until he starts shredding up a storm of blues licks and huge bends. It definitely takes you on a journey.

These are all tools for the toolbelt, sometimes you gotta use different tools. Different songs will ask you to use different tools. There are no hard and fast rules. Do what feels right for the song.

Here are some more things to keep in mind…

- It likely won't come easy in the beginning
- You'll find that sometimes it does come easier… Other times you gotta break through a brick wall to find anything you feel works
- You will find some backing music is easier to write to than others
- Sometimes the solo will feel like it's writing itself
- Sometimes you'll love what you write
- Sometimes you'll hate what you write
- A lot of the time, you'll like what you've written, but after playing it over and over so many times, you think it may now be boring. But that's just because you are too close to it, you've just played and heard it hundreds of times in a row, of course you're sick of it! 😛
- An easy way to start is to begin on a target note for the key.

A few more thoughts...

- Think about what kind of FEEL you want your solo to have. Do you have it seem happy, sad, energetic, aggressive, or something else?
- Leave space. While you are the "lead" part, it's your job to make the backing music sound good.
- Take your listener on a journey, think of a roller coaster, it has ups, downs, loops and all sorts. It's not just going to take you in a straight line the whole ride.

When you get stuck...

- Take a break, get up, grab a beverage, let your mind wander. After 10 minutes or so, pick your guitar back up and see if inspiration strikes. If not, pick it back up tomorrow.
- Or... put the pressure on. Some of my best solos were written hours before heading into the studio to record them (not good for the stress levels though!).

This Week's Practice

1. Memorize the blues scales (by simply memorizing where the "Blues note" is added for each of the pentatonic scale patterns) You must be able to add it and take it out when you want to. In other worlds the blues note cannot be permanently fixed into the scale patterns you have learned. It's an optional extra, for when you want to use it.

2. Improvise using the blues scales in both MAJOR and MINOR keys in different keys using ALL of the blues jam tracks you can find in the "Tools" section of the members area.

This Week's Challenge

Write a guitar solo to the "A Straight Rhythm" blues jam track you can find in the "tools" section of the members area.

Your solo MUST:

- Be the same every time you play it
- Last for AT LEAST 12 Bars (one round of the 12 bar blues)
- Use a minimum of 3 scale patterns

Record yourself playing your solo and upload a video into the private facebook community.

Optional For The Overachievers:

Make your solo last for 36 bars (3 times through the 12 bar blues. Use all 5 scale patterns and include high fret notes (AKA scale patterns above the 12th fret).

CHAPTER #6

If you've missed any info or are still a bit unsure from the last 5 chapters, please go back and make sure you understand everything up to here - it's crucial to your success as a guitar player.

Seriously, if you continue from this point without understanding the previous 5 chapters, you are literally wasting your time.

The only people who don't have success with the GPR System™ are people who will read through the information without actually putting it to work.

This book is an ACTIVE book, you need to be picking up your guitar, putting in the work, going over the patterns again and again.

If you're not willing to do that. Stop wasting your time right now and throw this book in the bin, because that's all it'll be good for.

This book isn't intended to be entertainment for you, for you to say to yourself "Ah! Is that how it works!" while never actually applying it on the guitar. It's designed to make you be able to play guitar in a way you always wanted to.

It's like buying weights and a training program, reading through the exercises, then just looking at the weights and wondering why you don't have a 6-pack yet…

This book puts understanding the fretboard into the simplest, easiest to understand, easiest to memorize way I've ever seen.

So if you're not going to implement this information, then you'll never be the guitarist you want to be, and will always be one of those guys or gals that say to yourself… "I'll get into it one day".

So stop, right now, and have a reality check with yourself.

Do you understand the information in the previous chapters? If not, go back and revise over them until you do. If you HAVE been spending a week on each chapter and still don't have a firm understanding… THAT IS OK! All I ask is that you put in 110% effort.

Some students have said they have found it easier to make it into a 20-week program, spending 2 weeks on each chapter. There is no right or wrong way, as long as you keep building this knowledge up in the GPR System™ brick by brick.
I have good news…

If you have been paying attention and putting in the work so far, and have had some killer wins with your guitar playing already, you are going to love where we are going next.

With the thousands of guitar players who have learned the GPR System™, and the amazing results they have got with their guitar playing, I KNOW this system will (and already is) working for you.

We're now going to pour more gasoline on the fire. You're going to love what's coming in this chapter.

Before we do, a quick note on why revising over the previous chapters, even if you have been putting in the work the whole way, is so important…

Going through this book more than once is very beneficial because there's so much information you would have gathered, and now you have a better understanding, you'll be able to see all the information with a new perspective

It's not because you missed anything…It's not that you didn't notice it the first time…It's that there's something **in you** that wasn't there the first time you read the book. As your understanding and awareness of the GPR System™ grows, the more information you will see as you revise over the previous chapters.

Diatonic Scale Patterns

In this chapter we start diving into the full Major scale, "the Diatonic scale". And just like we did in the previous chapter with the blues scale, we're simply adding notes into the patterns you already know and building upon the "Skeleton".

We've covered two types of scales so far, the Pentatonic scale, and the Blues scale. Now that we're shifting into focusing on the Diatonic scale, we're going to work on them for the remainder of the chapters. Because the Diatonic scale is the key to unlock everything else we need to know on the fretboard, including the modes.

Once we've covered the diatonic scales, you'll be able to play along to any track in Major or Minor keys, AND you'll be able to use the modes to force specific sounds from your soloing, we'll get to that in a second…

You'll see as we work through these patterns, they're all based on the Pentatonic patterns you've already learned. Here's a quick glance at the patterns before we dive in deeper.
Look at the notes showing what color dot represents what kind of note… If you focus on the Red, Blue and Black notes, you'll see that they are just the pentatonic scale patterns you already know. Now adding in the diatonic notes (shown as black hollow circles) we are playing the full major 'Diatonic' scale patterns.

Take a quick look at all of the patterns below and wrap your mind around the fact that all we are doing is adding a few notes to the patterns you already know... Then move on to the next pages and we'll go through each pattern one-by-one.

Memorize The Diatonic Scale Patterns

 = Major Root Note   ● = Pentatonic Note

 = Minor Root Note   ○ = Added Diatonic Note

C Diatonic Pattern
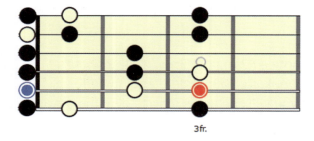
3fr.

A Diatonic Pattern
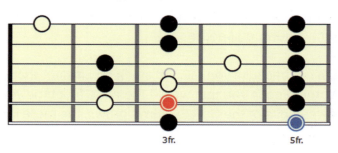
3fr.   5fr.

G Diatonic Pattern
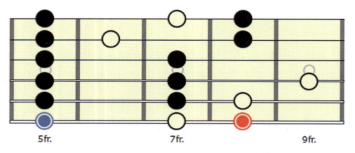
5fr.   7fr.   9fr.

E Diatonic Pattern
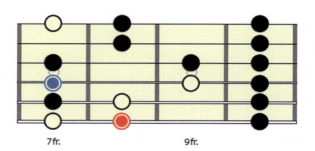
7fr.   9fr.

D Diatonic Pattern
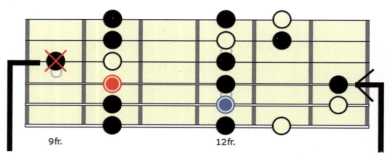
9fr.   12fr.

C Diatonic Pattern
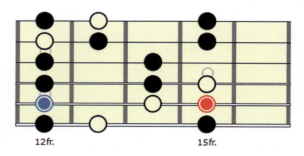
12fr.   15fr.

This note from the pentatonic pattern is no longer played here. To Make it easier for the Diatonic pattern, we play the exact same note a string higher over here...

Remember to take your time memorizing the new patterns, you have 5 to memorize and can use the whole week to really lock them in.

The major and minor root notes don't change, they stay the same as when we were working with just the pentatonic scales.

And you want to remember, just like with the blues scale patterns... You want to be able to add in the diatonic notes when you want to use them, and also be able to take them away when you don't want to use them (AKA when you want to stick to pentatonic playing).

When I first learned the Diatonic scale patterns, my first thought was... *"Well if there are more notes I can use in the Diatonic scale patterns, then why didn't I just learn those in the first place and forget about the Pentatonic scale patterns altogether!?"...*

The Pentatonic scale patterns are by far, the most usable scale patterns you will learn. They will work in almost every situation you'll ever come across. They are home base, the most important notes (generally) in a key.

As the years have gone by, I've found myself using the Diatonic notes less and focusing more on the Pentatonic notes. It all comes down to what the song is going to ask of you.

Just know that my assumption when I first learned the Diatonic scale patterns is completely wrong.

Think about it like this...

The Pentatonic scale patterns are like a hallway, and the blues note is a door we added off that hallway, a room we can go into with it's own feel, it's own mood. The Diatonic scale patterns are now going to open up a whole bunch of new rooms, new feels, new moods that we can explore... And we will always use the Pentatonic scale patterns to get to those rooms.

Now let's jump in, you're going to love this...

I've only been playing for 3 years, so I wasn't sure in the beginning that this was too much for me, or I wasn't qualified enough... If you are interested and serious about playing the guitar, and enjoy it as much as I have... It's amazing. **The fretboard has come alive. The patterns, the diatonic, blues, all the modes.**

- **Jim Stewart**, *Michigan, USA*

Memorize The "C" Diatonic Scale Pattern

First up, we'll dive into the C Shape Diatonic pattern. So far (for the most part) the scale patterns we've learned have only been 2 notes per string, however, with the diatonic patterns, a lot of the time we'll be playing 3 notes per string.

The **Major** and **Minor** root notes for this pattern are in the same place as they've always been so that's nothing new.

"C" Diatonic Scale Pattern

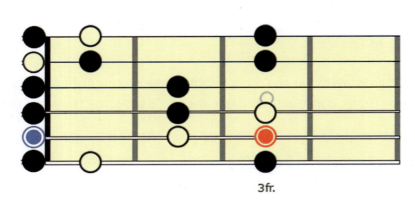

Memorize The "A" Diatonic Scale Pattern

The next pattern is the "A" diatonic scale pattern.

Again, this contains all of the notes from the "A" pentatonic scale pattern but we have the extra notes in here from the major scale that makes it Diatonic. You may be wondering about what fingers to use for this pattern, as it spans over 5 frets, and to your count, you only have 4 fingers… Our index finger is going to do double duty here, stretch that finger over to the first fret in this position to get that diatonic note on the high E string.

"A" Diatonic Scale Pattern

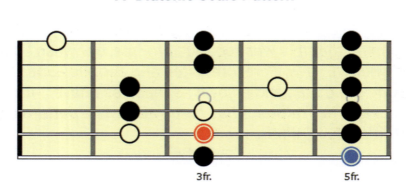

Memorize The "G" Diatonic Scale Pattern

This is your *"G" shape "Anchor"* but now it contains the extra notes which you'll be learning how to use in the upcoming chapters. This pattern also spans across 5 frets, so use your pinky to stretch over and get the note on the 9th fret of the D string.

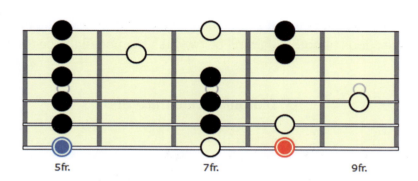

"G" Diatonic Scale Pattern

Memorize The "E" Diatonic Scale Pattern

I always felt this pattern feels to my fingers like a mixture of the C and A diatonic scale shapes, so really make sure you focus in on this one to get it right. Half of this pattern is exactly the same. On 3 of the strings (Low E, A and High E) you're playing with exactly the same fingers.

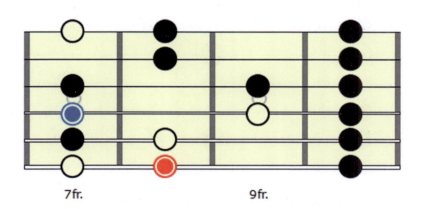

"E" Diatonic Scale Pattern

Memorize The "D" Diatonic Scale Pattern

Last one! This one is really easy because we are going to move where we play one of the Pentatonic notes (don't let the diagram fool you, this is really easy).

The first diagram below shows the note we are usually playing on the G string, and how we are moving it to the D string to make it more in line with the rest of the pattern.

The reason we can do this is because these 2 positions on the fretboard are the exact same note (try it out for yourself!). So have a look at both diagrams below, then memorize the second diagram from the D Diatonic scale pattern.

"D" Diatonic Scale Pattern

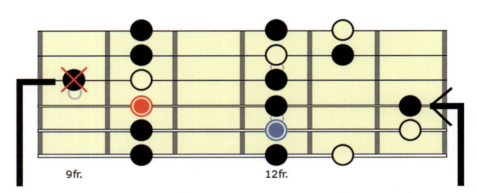

This note from the pentatonic pattern is no longer played here. To make it easier for the Diatonic pattern, we play the exact same note a string higher over here...

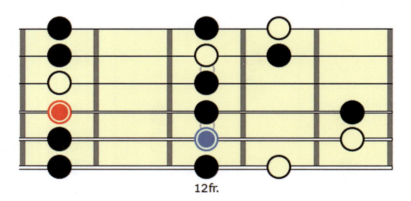

This is the only scale pattern that's slightly different from the pentatonic shape, but only by a single note, and the note is EXACTLY the same as I mentioned before.

All of these Diatonic scale patterns, just like the Pentatonic scale patterns, are moveable. Meaning we can change these patterns to be in any key that we want. It's also why in the diagram below showing the fretboard up to the 15th fret, you'll see the "C" pattern in 2 places, because these patterns use the CAGED system just like the Pentatonic patterns.

So there you have it - the 5 Diatonic Scale Patterns!

Now here's the complete "Skeleton" WITH the added Diatonic notes. After you have taken time to memorize each "Jigsaw Piece", you can easily play every single one of these notes on your guitar, almost without thinking (and eventually, definitely without thinking about it).

Take a look at the diagram below, and reflect for a moment on just how much you have learned so far. Congratulations on your hard work, because now, look at how much this fretboard makes sense to you (and this picture will become clearer and clearer as we continue on)…

 = Major Root Note   ◯ = Added Diatonic Note

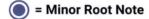 = Minor Root Note

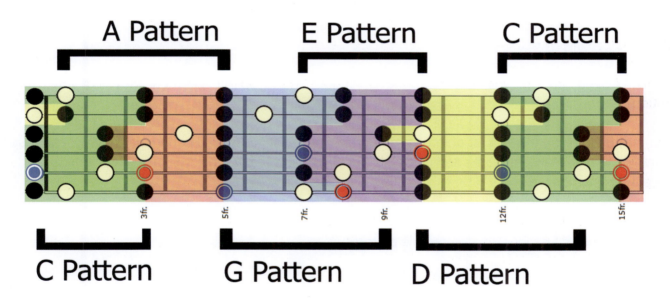

Now you can see that when you're soloing round the fretboard you have so many more notes you can choose, and this doesn't mean you have to play all of them 😉

These are tools… So pay close attention to this next part.

What Scales Do I Use?

If you were a builder, you wouldn't turn up to the job with just a hammer, you wouldn't turn up with just a saw… You'd bring BOTH because you might need them.

And you might also need a screwdriver…

It's best to think of these scales as **totally different things.** Different tools. So when you go to play a solo you can think, "Hmmm, Should I use the hammer, the saw, or the screwdriver?"

They each do different jobs, they each do different things…

If there's a piece of music that'll work better using the pentatonic scale and you start using the diatonic scale, it'll be a lot harder to get the job done… Just as it's harder to hammer in a nail using a screwdriver, right?

Sometimes there are tools designed to do a specific job and everyone knows, if you wanna put a nail in somewhere, you use a hammer. You wanna screw a screw in, you use a screwdriver. You want to cut a piece of wood, you'll need a saw. I can't imagine it's easy chopping wood with a screwdriver…

They each do different things…

We'll dive deep into what scales to choose later, for now, I want you to experiment with all of your options.

You may be thinking this is a lot of info to memorize, and yes it is. I'm also confident you've got this! So I want you to really take your time and play with 1 diatonic pattern per day for 5 days. Then in 5 days you'll have them memorized.

And I bet if you start with your G+3 pattern and add in the diatonic notes, you'll see, very quickly, just how easy it is to play all of these diatonic scale patterns.

What About Theory?

Well, remember how the actual SCALES live inside of the SCALE PATTERNS when you were learning the pentatonic patterns? The same is true for the diatonic patterns.

And again, **2 different things** we have **"SCALE PATTERNS"** and we have **"SCALES"**.

What we do using the GPR System™ is learn the scale patterns because that shows us the notes we can play over the entire fretboard. If you never read this next page but just memorized and played from the patterns, you'd still be playing all the available notes in any given key…
But there is real power in knowing exactly where these patterns come from.

So now we're going to focus on the scales inside of the patterns because knowing those will help you hit better notes while you are soloing.

In **Major** or **Minor** the target notes for the diatonic scales are the same target notes from the pentatonic scales, but this is a bit different from playing to the chord changes, which we cover a bit later.

If you have the optional video course that goes along with this book, I highly recommend you go and check that out for this next part. Either way, pay close attention and grab a piece of paper to take notes on as we go through this next part…

The Major Scale Formula

We use a formula to get the full major scale. It's simple, easy to memorize and easy to understand.

The full *'Major Scale Formula'* is the following:

Tone, Tone, Semitone, Tone, Tone, Tone, Semitone

Tone = Moving up 2 frets on your guitar (I.e. From the 5th fret to the 7th fret)
Semitone = Moving up 1 fret on your guitar (I.e. From the 5th fret to the 6th fret)

You want to memorize this formula, even if it makes no sense to you right now, it will very soon.

We use letters to show scale formulas. A capital **T** to show a TONE and a lowercase **s** to show semitone (since it's a smaller shift).

T = Tone
s = Semitone

So we have: **T T s T T T s**

2 Tones, 1 Semitone, 3 Tones, 1 Semitone

And just like how the CAGED system links back in on itself, so does every scale formula so the major scale formula could look like this...

$$T\,T\,s\,T\,T\,T\,s\,T\,T\,s\,\mathbf{\underline{T\,T\,T\,s\,T\,T\,s}}\,T\,T\,T\,s\,T\,T\,s\,T\,T\,T\,s$$

In the key of "C" the major scale formula gives us these notes (with the formula in between to show the distance we are traveling). Remember the key of "C" is the easiest to visually see as there are no sharps or flats.

Remember the T's and s's are the scale formula, the larger letters are the notes of the scale.

$$C\,_T\,D\,_T\,E\,_s\,F\,_T\,G\,_T\,A\,_T\,B\,_s\,C$$

You can test this out on your guitar by grabbing a C note on the 3rd fret of the A string on your guitar (seriously, grab your guitar right now and follow along).

- Play the C note on the 3rd fret of the A string, then move up a **Tone** to the 5th fret of the A string, which is a D note.
- Move up another **Tone** to the 7th fret, which is an E note.
- Next we move up a **semitone** (aka 1 fret) to get an F note on the 8th fret.
- Then a **Tone** up to the G note on the 10th fret of the A string.
- Another **Tone** up to the 12th fret, which is an A note.
- Move a **Tone** up to the 14th fret, which is a B note.
- And then to complete the full major scale, we move up a **semitone** to the 15th fret, which is of course, a C note.

Following through the above bullet points, you just played a full C Major scale.
So if there are 7 notes in a scale, why did we just play 8 notes? That is because for a scale to sound 'complete' we need to get to 'home' again which is the root note, the note we started the scale on. Try playing through the pattern again, but stop on the B note... Every inch of your body would be SCREAMING for you to complete the scale and play the next C note to relieve the tension of sitting on an unresolved note.

Each note in the scale can be paired with a number like this:

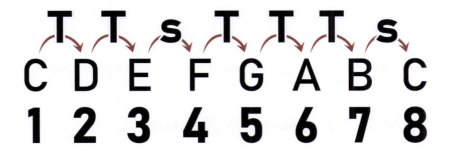

The 8th note is really "1" because it is the beginning on the next scale an octave higher (same note, just higher).

When we play a diatonic patterns we just play the scale the same way as we played the pentatonic patterns, from "C" to "C" but this time, we play all of the notes from the diatonic (full major) scale because the patterns have us playing all of those notes automatically.

If we wanted to play a minor diatonic scale, we start on the minor root note and play through 7 more notes to reach the octave.

Here's an example in the key of A minor:

$$A\ _T\ B\ _s\ C\ _T\ D\ _T\ E\ _s\ F\ _T\ G\ _T\ A$$

Remember that the scale patterns do ALL of the work for us, this is just letting you know the work that they ARE doing.

To keep it simple... Just position the major or minor root notes into the key you want, just like you would with the pentatonic patterns (they are the same notes after all), and you are good to go in that key. You'll notice that the scale formula we learned before looks different in the minor example above, that's just because we started from a different starting point.

To have this make complete sense, look at the C note, then follow along with the scale formula and wrap back around to the beginning. You'll notice it still works in a T T s T T T s fashion. Remember the Tones and semitone are not the notes, they are the distance between the notes.
If you need more clarity on this, read this through a few times, play through the examples on your guitar and if you have the optional video course, go through that to really lock things in.

We'll be diving deeper into this subject next week.

What Notes Can I Bend?

You can begin on any note that lies within the scale pattern and bend it up, but it's important that you know where you are actually bending to.

Think of bends as slides. If you were going to slide up to a note, you'd make sure that you would be sliding into a note that was still in key, right? Same thing with bending notes.

There are two main types of bends. **FULL bends** and **HALF bends.**

Full bends are bending up a Tone (AKA 2 frets). Half bends are bending up a semitone (AKA 1 fret). Have a look at the diagram that links up the whole fretboard in this chapter and see where you can bend to.

An example to get you going... In the key of C Major/A minor, you can bend the 7th fret of the high string up a half bend (so it sounds like the 8th fret) and you can bend the 8th fret up a full bend (so it sounds like the 10th fret).

A good exercise to get your bends to be in pitch, is to play the note you want to bend to (E.g. If you are practicing a full bend, play 2 frets higher than the fret you are going to bend from), then do the bend and make it sound like the note you just played. Go back and forth with this exercise for a few minutes everyday until you feel confident your bends are in tune and going to the right places.

*I've been playing guitar since 1970 on and off. I've taken some private lessons at $20 per half hour and they were good, very good... But I've learned more in the last year that I've been a member of Guitar Mastery Method than I have in any of those other lessons. I now have a really good understanding of the CAGED system, I have a really good understanding of the modes, I have ALL the tools I need. All in all, this is probably **the best 10 weeks I've ever spent.***

- **Irwin H. Zaetz**, *Connecticut, USA*

This Week's Practice

1. Memorize the Diatonic Scale Patterns (by adding the extra notes shown in the scale diagrams to the pentatonic patterns you already know). You must be able to add them in and take them out when you like. In other words, the diatonic notes cannot be permanently fixed into the pentatonic scale patterns you have learned. They must be two separate things in your mind.

2. Use the scale memorization exercises I taught you in chapter #1 for the Diatonic Scale Patterns.

3. If you have the optional 10-Week Master The Fretboard video course to go along with this book, review over the lesson, in particular the "Major Scale Theory" section at least THREE times taking notes with pen and paper. It's important that you have this theory memorized. You should be able to teach this to someone else before starting the next chapter.

4. Practice improvising using the Diatonic Scale Patterns. Focus on bending notes that you "can" bend to (AKA, bending to notes still within the scale).

This Week's Challenge

Improvise using the Diatonic Scale Patterns, playing as **_FAST_** as you can. Record & upload it into the Facebook community. Why **_FAST_**?

I want to STRESS out your mind. Trying to scramble and find the new notes while playing fast may seem totally frustrating while you're playing, but what's happening in your mind is the important thing. Putting your mind under pressure like this forces the memory of the notes to be stronger.

It's like saying to your brain *"Hey! Memorize these notes, they're super important!"* After doing this, when you put your guitar down, your mind will go to work making your memory of the diatonic scale patterns stronger.

That's all for this week, so make sure you experiment using the G+3 Diatonic pattern through a bunch of different keys both Major and Minor and I'll see you in chapter #7!

CHAPTER #7

We're here! The beginning of "The Modes"... Now we're not diving in and playing them this week (although, as you'll find out soon enough, you actually already are playing two of them) but we are going to lay the foundation.

So take a breath, apart from some memorization for the modes, we're going to be taking it a bit easier this week to let those diatonic scale patterns sink in even more.

Once again you want to make sure you've completed the previous 6 chapters so this makes sense to you. It's all progressing and adding onto each chapter. You'll want to memorize what these names are and what type of scale they are. We'll get you playing the modes in the next chapter.

What Are "The Modes"?

The modes are just different "moods", different feelings and different flavors. Think of major and minor, they sound very different and have a very different feeling.

For instance, 'Here Comes The Sun' by The Beatles has a very positive & uplifting feeling, not just in the words, but in the music itself. That's because it's in a major key, A major to be exact. Now think of 'Stairway To Heaven' by Led Zeppelin. It has a very different "mood"... Melancholic & reflective. That's because it's in a minor key, A minor to be exact.

Both these songs are in "A", one if major and one is minor and they have two totally different "Moods". In fact, they are actually in two of "The Modes".

That's how you want to think about the modes, because it's a really simple concept, but the fancy names can give the illusion that it's actually complicated... It's really not.

I once said on a live lesson "The Modes take 20 minutes to learn and 2 years to believe what you learned is actually true". I said that because that was my experience with them, I thought... "Surely it's not that simple"...
It is.

So as we go forward, remember to look at what's right in front of your nose, instead of trying to see mountains in the distance. All the work we have done up to this point has set you up to "unlock" the modes, not learn them.

You already have learned them, all we are going to be doing in the chapters covering the modes is simply show you how to see them.

The only step you need to take before you can unlock the modes in your own mind is to memorize the 7 modes. In the chart below, you'll see a number, a name (that comes from the Greek language) and a quality (major, minor, diminished). You must memorize these all together, so if I asked you what #3 was, you could tell me that it was Phrygian and that it is a minor mode. If I asked you what Mixolydian is, you would be able to tell me it was #5 and it is a major mode.

Pay extra attention to Ionian and Aeolian as you must remember these are the "NATURAL Major" and "NATURAL minor". Here's a tip for you: 7 notes per scale, and 7 modes… There are also 7 days in a week so you can memorize 1 per day for the week.

Memorize The Modes

1	Ionian	Natural MAJOR
2	Dorian	minor
3	Phrygian	minor
4	Lydian	MAJOR
5	Mixolydian	MAJOR
6	Aeolian	Natural minor
7	Locrian	Diminished

That's all we're covering to do with the modes right now. Do whatever you need to do to get these memorized, write it on your arm, on the wall, on the windscreen of your car… Whatever it takes (just don't blame me for the repercussions!).

I can't thank you enough for your teaching methods. They're very simple, they're easy to follow, I was able to really grasp a hold of the concepts and go through each of the weeks… **Now I can play all over the whole fretboard, I know all of the pentatonic, diatonic, blues scales and patterns.** *And I'm just really excited about where that's going to take me next…*

- **Jon Michelson**, *Nebraska, USA*

Diatonic Scale Licks That Link The Patterns Together

Here are 4 Diatonic licks to help you blend the Diatonic scale patterns together. Something I want you to be aware of is HOW these patterns are linking up using the licks.

Diatonic Solo Licks

This Week's Practice

1. Memorize "The Modes" information. It's EXTREMELY important you have this locked in 100% before next week. Go over it every morning and every night before you go to sleep. You need to know it well so that if I call "#3", you can tell me exactly what mode it is and if it's major, minor, or diminished. For example: If I said "what number is Dorian?" You'd have to know what number that is.

2. Improvise using the diatonic scale patterns in many different keys. Search on Youtube to find more jam tracks in all different styles (Major and Minor).

3. Explore the "Diatonic Solo Licks" and move around in different ways to start to create a complete "grid" in your mind instead of just pattern-pattern-pattern (it will always feel like 5 patterns to some degree, so don't stress too much here.)

This Week's Challenges

Part #1: Record a video of yourself talking through the modes information after you've memorized it and upload it into the members community and DON'T CHEAT, you must have this information memorized and cannot read off a sheet.

Part #2: Search up the guitar tabs to some of your favorite solos and discover what type of scales they're using... Pentatonic, Diatonic, Blues or a mix of them. Try 3 songs. Some solos are easier to spot than others in the beginning. Post your findings into the members community... (E.g. The solo to the song ____ by the band ____ uses the ____ Scale pattern in the key of ___)

Here's two examples to get you started:

- The solo to the song **Paranoid** by the band **Black Sabbath** uses the **Pentatonic** Scale pattern in the key of **E minor**
- The solo to the song **Sweet Child O' Mine** by the band **Guns N' Roses** uses the **Diatonic** Scale pattern in the key of **Eb minor**

Part #3: Find a backing track in your favorite style on Youtube. Write a guitar solo that lasts a minimum of 45 seconds. With at least 15 seconds using pentatonic scales, 15 seconds using blues scales, and 15 seconds using the diatonic scales. **THIS IS NOT IMPROVISATION**... It's time to write another solo. Upload 2 videos to prove you're playing the same thing each time.

That wraps up Chapter #7 - Keep up the good work, you're really making progress now!

CHAPTER #8

We've covered A LOT of ground so far and you need to make sure you've been through the previous chapters because, as you know by now, they build upon each other.

If you attempt this without the previous chapters & lessons under your belt it will get frustrating and confusing. We don't want any hold ups, we want momentum. So go back if you need to. Even if you want to take a week right now and just recap over everything we have covered so far, that's ok.

There's still a bit to learn when it comes to the modes but right now we're going to keep it fairly simple. There's some crucial info in this chapter that's crucial to your success.

How To Play The Modes

We play the modes using the diatonic scale. In the Diatonic scale we have Major and Minor but there are other names for these particular scales.

We have 7 notes per scale, and we also have 7 modes.

You'll notice the first mode is called **Ionian**, this is **the Natural Major.**

Ionian is the **Natural Major** because this is the scale we've been playing to when we say "C Major" for example. You'll also see that the 6th mode is called **Aeolian**, this is the **Natural minor**, so anytime we've been playing in "Minor" using the diatonic scale patterns, we've actually been playing Aeolian.

Remember how we have relative Majors and minors? Like how C Major and A minor both use the EXACT same notes?

Starting from a "C" means we're in the key of C Major, and starting from a different starting point, the A note, we're in the key of A minor.

So if you didn't learn anything else at all from this point on... You'd already know how to play 2 of the 7 modes. Ionian and Aeolian. Two different ways of playing the diatonic scale, two different feels, 2 different moods.

Remember how I told you this was easy? I'll repeat this again... You have already been playing 2 of the 7 modes anytime you have been using the diatonic scale pattern.

So, How Do We Learn The Other 5 Modes?

It's simple, every other note in the scale can be used as a starting point, just like with Ionian (Natural Major) and Aeolian (Natural minor).

The best part? The diatonic scale patterns have already done the hard work for us.

I recommend that before you pick up your guitar and use the modes that are hiding in the diatonic scale patterns, we start out by learning the modes on paper. After you've got that sorted, we can very easily apply these to the guitar.

The Modes On Paper

Read through this next section a few times to soak in this information. One single line is easy to read fast, but please stop and soak in every single sentence in this next section. Because this is really simple to understand, and very easy to overthink it.

There are 7 notes in the major scale, each note represents a starting point for a different mode.

1. Ionian
2. Dorian
3. Phrygian
4. Lydian
5. Mixolydian
6. Aeolian
7. Locrian

Now, in the key of C Major the 7 notes are in the dark color below. Ignore the light grey letters (which are the same notes anyway):

C D E F G A B **C D E F G A B** C D E F G A B

So if we want to play a C Ionian scale, we start on the C note and play through the notes until we loop back around to the '1' (aka C).

If we took that same series of notes, and started on the A note, we have gone through the same notes, starting from a different note, and thus playing in A Aeolian (Natural minor):

C D E F G A B C D E F G **A B C D E F G** A B

Remember how each mode has a number? Well now let's add in numbers underneath the notes of the scale.

We've gone back to C Ionian (Natural Major). See how C is listed as "1", D is listed as "2", etc?

Also notice that the grayed out notes and numbers either side of the darker text is an exact replica. It is the exact same "scale" and this is showing you how the scale is infinite in both directions. It just keeps linking back onto itself.

Ionian:

C	D	E	F	G	A	B	**C**	**D**	**E**	**F**	**G**	**A**	**B**	C	D	E	F	G	A	B
1	2	3	4	5	6	7	**1**	**2**	**3**	**4**	**5**	**6**	**7**	1	2	3	4	5	6	7

So just as starting on #1 and playing through the scale is playing Ionian, and starting on #6 and playing through the scale is Aeolian (the two modes you already know how to play)...

If we start on #2 and play through the scale, we will be playing a Dorian scale:

Dorian:

C	D	E	F	G	A	B	C	**D**	**E**	**F**	**G**	**A**	**B**	**C**	D	E	F	G	A	B
1	2	3	4	5	6	7	1	**2**	**3**	**4**	**5**	**6**	**7**	**1**	2	3	4	5	6	7

If we start on #3 and play through the scale, we will be playing a Phrygian scale:

Phrygian:

C	D	E	F	G	A	B	C	D	**E**	**F**	**G**	**A**	**B**	**C**	**D**	E	F	G	A	B
1	2	3	4	5	6	7	1	2	**3**	**4**	**5**	**6**	**7**	**1**	**2**	3	4	5	6	7

If we start on #4 and play through the scale, we will be playing a Lydian scale:

Lydian:

C	D	E	F	G	A	B	C	D	E	**F**	**G**	**A**	**B**	**C**	**D**	**E**	F	G	A	B
1	2	3	4	5	6	7	1	2	3	**4**	**5**	**6**	**7**	**1**	**2**	**3**	4	5	6	7

Starting on #5 and playing through the scale, you will be playing a Mixolydian scale:

Mixolydian:

Of course the next scale, we are already familiar with, the "Natural minor" starts on #6::

Aeolian:

Moving up one more, to start on #7 and playing through the scale, we have a Locrian scale.

Locrian:

Of course to complete a single scale and have it sound 'resolved' we'd play one more note (for instance, in the Locrian example above, we'd play one more "B" note to complete the whole octave or else it will feel unresolved).

So when we position the scale patterns on the fretboard in the Natural major key of C, not only do we have the relative minor (Aeolian) of A, we have a whole list of modes we can play.

1. **"C" Ionian**
2. **"D" Dorian**
3. **"E" Phrygian**
4. **"F" Lydian**
5. **"G" Mixolydian**
6. **"A" Aeolian**
7. **"B" Locrian**

The Modal Formulas

The reason why these scales sound different, have different names and make us feel different when we hear them, is because the 'Scale Formula' is different for each of them.

Remember that the diatonic scale patterns have already done all of this hard work for us, as long as you understand the concept that the formulas are different for each mode, you're good to go.

You don't have to be thinking about these formulas while you're playing. Think of it as if I was showing you how to turn on a light. I say… "Hey, to turn on the light, just flick the light switch". Do you need to know what goes on behind the wall to make the light go on? No. But if you wanted to know WHY the light turns on when you flick the switch, then we'd dig a little deeper, that's what we're doing here.

Just remember, that after you have gone through this section, the light will still turn on when you flick the switch even if you are a bit hazy on what's happening behind the wall.

In this instance, the light switch for us are the diatonic scale patterns (remember, I said they've already done the hard work for us) and what's behind the wall to make it work, is this explanation right now.

Remember when we covered the "Full Major Scale Formula"? This is the exact same thing.

Here is the Key of C Major with the modal numbers added below the notes:

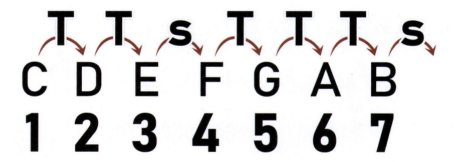

Playing through these same 7 notes, but starting and ending on a different note will change the mode we're in. This is because the scale formula is different for each mode.

T T s T T T s - is the scale formula for the Natural Major scale (Ionian Mode)

Remember that the **Tones** and **semitones** aren't the notes themselves, they are the *distance* between the notes.

Here's a visual representation of the modal formulas, just the same way as we visualized the modes themselves just before:

Ionian Modal Formula

T T s T T T s **T T s T T T s** T T s T T T s

Following this formula will take us from a note, in our previous example "C", all the way through the notes D, E, F, G, A, B and back to C an octave higher. This modal formula is the exact same formula as the full major scale formula you have already learned.

Now if we move up, and walk through the scale formula starting one step higher, we now have the modal formula for the 2nd mode, Dorian:

Dorian Modal Formula

T T s T T T s **T s T T T s T** T s T T T s

To get the other scale formulas, we just move up one step at a time…

Phrygian Modal Formula

T T s T T T s T T **s T T T s T T** s T T T s

Lydian Modal Formula

T T s T T T s T T s **T T T s T T s** T T T s

Mixolydian Modal Formula

T T s T T T s T T s T **T T s T T s T** T T s

Aeolian (Natural minor) **Modal Formula**

T T s T T T s T T s T T **T s T T s T T** T s

Locrian Modal Formula

T T s T T T s T T s T T T **s T T s T T T** s

You do not need to memorize all of these modal formulas, because they all live inside the Full Major Scale Formula you have already learned, and they are already implemented in the diatonic scale patterns you know.

Here's another way to visually see the different modal formulas. Grab your guitar and play through each of these modes following the modal formulas.

Use the same starting note (I recommend trying "G", the 3rd fret on the low E string) and see how as you change the Modal Scale Formula, the feeling and sound of the scale changes.

Remember: With a **Tone** you move up 2 frets (from 3rd fret to 5th fret) and with a **semitone** you move up 1 fret (from 3rd fret to 4th fret).

Mode	Modal Scale Formula
1. Ionian	T T S T T T S
2. Dorian	T S T T T S T
3. Phrygian	S T T T S T T
4. Lydian	T T T S T T S
5. Mixolydian	T T S T T S T
6. Aeolian	T S T T S T T
7. Locrian	S T T S T T T

Simply by starting on different notes and going through a different modal formula creates a different mode with different characteristics/mood/flavor.

If you're having trouble getting a grasp on this information, don't worry, you're not alone. Many people need to go through the information multiple times before it finally "clicks". So if you're still struggling, go grab a coffee and come back and read through all of this again.

If it still doesn't make sense, sit on it overnight, come back tomorrow with a fresh perspective and go through it again.

When you first get this information dropped on you, it can feel like trying to drink from a fire hose, so take your time and just let this soak in. Remember, it's easy… Once the lightbulb turns on, it never goes out.

Now, we can work out the other keys and how they fit into the modes. And the way we will do this is literally by writing the modes out "on paper".

Grab a spare piece of paper & a pen, then copy this down:

T	T	s	T	T	T	s
1	2	3	4	5	6	7

Then, choose a starting note. We're gonna do the key of 'E Ionian' and follow the scale formula to find all the notes in E Ionian (Natural Major).

Step #1: Place the note you want onto the number associated with the mode you want. In this case, Ionian is #1, so we place E under #1:

Step #2: Find the next note by moving either a 'Tone' or 'Semitone' up the musical alphabet (depending on what the modal formula is asking you to do). In this instance, we move a 'Tone' from E up to F#.

Step #3 - 7: Continue adding in the notes the modal formula is asking you to add until the scale formula will link you back round to the note you began with (in this case, E).

T	T	s	T	T	T	s
1	2	3	4	5	6	7
E	F#	G#	A	B	C#	D#

Notice how at number 7 we have D#, and a semitone up from D# is E (which means we are looping back around to the start).

This is how you can tell if you have made a mistake when working out notes in a scale/mode, if it doesn't link back around to itself, then somewhere along the way you've put in a wrong note.

This is good because we have a teacher sitting there telling us we got it right or wrong simply by seeing if it works or not.

Now in the previous example, all of the notes that make up with the numbers 1 to 7 show you the different starting points for different modes.

In the Key of E Ionian, we can also play, for example, G# Phryrgian because G# is on number 3.

We can play A Lydian etc...

Get a piece of paper and write out all of the keys from A to G# (12 in total). This will really help solidify this practice into your mind.

Working these out, like anything, will be challenging in the beginning. Keep practicing and eventually you'll be able to move away from the paper and work it all out in your head.

If you have the additional 10-Week Master The Fretboard video course then refer back to that for walkthrough demonstrations of this.

Working Out Modes

We don't always work out the modes starting from #1, Ionian. We can begin on any of the scale degrees and work through the scale formula.

For instance, if we wanted to work out the notes in E Phrygian, all we would need to do is put an E on number 3, then work through the scale formula. You'll see this as an example on the next page.

Then we have a few for you to try. Start on the note written down on one of the numbers, then continue through the scale formula to find all of the notes in that key/mode.

The Modes On Paper

	T		T		s		T		T		T		s
1		2		3		4		5		6		7	
C		D		E		F		G		A		B	

	T		T		s		T		T		T		s
1		2		3		4		5		6		7	
												F#	

	T		T		s		T		T		T		s
1		2		3		4		5		6		7	
						Gb							

	T		T		s		T		T		T		s
1		2		3		4		5		6		7	
		C											

	T		T		s		T		T		T		s
1		2		3		4		5		6		7	
								C#					

After you have completed these, grab a piece of paper (or use the next page which is left blank for you) and put down a random note onto a number, then work through the scale formula to get all the notes in that key/mode.

The Modes On Paper

```
        T       T       s       T       T       T       s
   1       2       3       4       5       6       7


        T       T       s       T       T       T       s
   1       2       3       4       5       6       7


        T       T       s       T       T       T       s
   1       2       3       4       5       6       7


        T       T       s       T       T       T       s
   1       2       3       4       5       6       7


        T       T       s       T       T       T       s
   1       2       3       4       5       6       7
```

Write out the scale formulas & numbers as above on your own piece of paper and continue this exercise.

This is "The Modes On Paper". Let this soak in, possibly for a day or two, then continue on and we'll put all of this knowledge to use on the guitar fretboard (this next part is really easy).

The Modes On Your Guitar

Now we are going to take your knowledge of the modes and show you how to play these modal scales on the guitar using the diatonic scale patterns you already know.

We're going to focus on the G Diatonic Scale Pattern to get this locked down.

Remember your 'Major Root Note' you memorize in the scale patterns? Have a look at the diagram below, you'll notice that it now has a "1" in it.

The "1", as you know, represents Ionian. Same thing as (Natural) Major, just a different name.

If you were to start on #1 and play through 7 more notes (for a total of 8 played notes), you would have played a full Ionian scale (remember, the scales are INSIDE of the patterns).

In the position of the diagram below, you would have played from a C, to another C walking through the major scale formula (T T s T T T s).

The Modes On Guitar

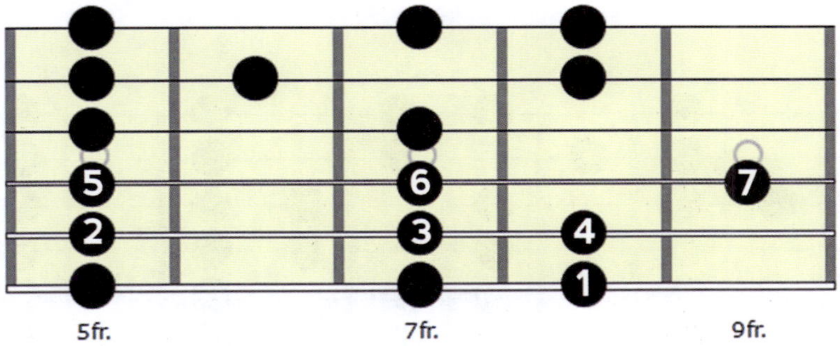

Here's the kicker...

To play any mode, just choose the mode you want to play, start on that number and play through a total of 8 notes. And you would have played a modal scale.

For instance, if you start on #3, which here lands on an E note, and played through 8 notes, you would have played an E Phrygian scale.

Stop right now and read through the previous two paragraphs, it really is that simple.

That's why we spent so much time laying the foundation for this, now it's as easy as 1 - 2 - 3.
1 (choose a mode) 2 (find the mode in the scale pattern) 3 (play it!).

Spend at least 15 minutes playing around with this, play through the different modal scales and see how they all feel different (some more than others).

The best part is that you don't have to focus on each modal scale formula, because the diatonic scale patterns take care of all of that for us.

All that work you did memorizing the scale patterns is now really paying off.

Using Other Patterns

The example on the previous page is the G Diatonic scale pattern, but you can use this same system for any of the diatonic scale patterns to play the modes.

For instance, if you wanted to use the C Diatonic scale pattern, then go to where you memorized the major root note, that is "1". Then as you play through the scale pattern, count as you play the notes. 1, 2, 3, 4, 5, 6, 7… You just located all 7 of the root notes for the modes within that scale pattern.

Go back and look at the G Diatonic scale pattern and do exactly that. If you don't have a guitar in your hands right now, just do it in your mind.

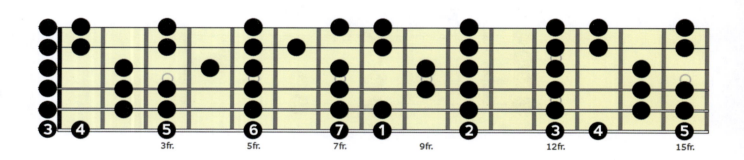

This diagram shows the starting notes for the modes (numbered) on the low E string.

Feeling lost? Just look at #1 and #6 and you'll see the major and minor root notes for the G pattern.

Grab the note for the mode you want to play and continue into the Diatonic scale pattern to continue to play the mode.

We've positioned these scale patterns in the key of C major, if you look at #1 and #6 you'll see the G shape pattern in the fretboard.

If I said, you wanna play a Mixolydian scale, then grab the #5 note on the Low E string and play through the vertical scale pattern. This is on the 3rd fret, so we'd be playing G Mixolydian.
This is just another way of organizing & finding the modes. Use whatever system you find the easiest.

We're going to dive deeper into the modes on guitar in the next chapter, but I want you to experiment with the modes along with the backing tracks in your members area.

For this week, just stick with using the modes with the scale patterns positioned right where they have been on all of the examples so far.

Remember that the scale patterns all link up to each other just like they always have, so by positioning ONE scale pattern into a mode, you have actually positioned ALL of the scale patterns into the mode.

In the next chapter, we will begin moving the modes around the fretboard.

This Week's Practice

1. Practice soloing in all different modes along with the supplied drone backing tracks (Found in your members area)

2. While you're improvising in the modes, find which notes sound good to hang on and which notes sound good as "Passing notes". These will change from mode to mode.

This Week's Challenges

Part #1: Complete the missing notes for the modes, upload them into the Facebook community.

Part #2: After you've practiced and got a feel for each mode, upload a video of you playing along to 2 of the following modes with the supplied backing tracks. Note: Spend a few days jamming on these to find the character of the mode before uploading.

Dorian
Phrygian
Lydian
Mixolydian

Great work. Next week I'm going to show you even more information you already know to do with what chords you can play in each key & mode (when I first realized this, it blew my mind!).

See you in chapter #9.

CHAPTER #9

Congrats! You've covered a huge amount of material so far! In this chapter we're going to discuss the little things to help make the modes more useful.

We're gonna learn to move the modes around the fretboard, chords in the key, mode flavors, and a quick hack to move across the fretboard easily, hitting the modal target notes giving you the purest sound of the mode - Let's dive in!

Mode Target Notes

When playing in modes, you want to target the "Chord Tones" and use the "Non-Chord Tones" as your passing notes.

The reason you don't JUST want to play "chord tones" is because the passing notes are the ones that add the real flavor.

For each mode, you have 3 Chord tones and 4 Non-Chord Tones.

Think of it like this - for each mode there are *3 target notes* and *4 passing notes*.

We can use the G Diatonic scale pattern (in the diagram shown) to find the chord tones and the non-chord tones. The chord tones are the notes from the "Triad" of the chord, and the non-chord tones are the rest of the notes in the scale.

How do you find the chord tones? Simply just use the 1st, 3rd, and 5th note of the scale.

So if we use Ionian (Natural Major) as an example, the numbers 1, 3 and 5 are the chord tones (target notes) and all the rest, 2, 3, 6, & 7, would be the passing notes.

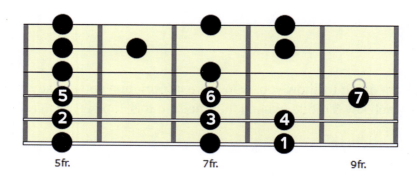

In this instance, with the G Diatonic scale pattern positioned on the 5th fret, we look at what the target notes are. All we do is ask... "What are 1, 3 and 5 landing on?"

The answer, in this case, C, E and G.

So we know the notes we should be aiming for are C, E and G all over the fretboard. (not just in this pattern). And we can use all of the other notes to add color/flavor.

One thing to remember with passing notes is, to get to a target note you can normally just go up or down one note in the pattern and you will land on a chord tone. UNLESS, you are on 6 or 7 where you have 2 passing tones next to each other.

Here's another example: Let's say we want to find the chord tones and non chord tones for E Phrygian. We start on the root note for Phrygian (which was covered in the last chapter) and we arrange the note numbers like this so that the Phrygian root note is now listed at #1 (this is just to find the chord tones & non-chord tones).

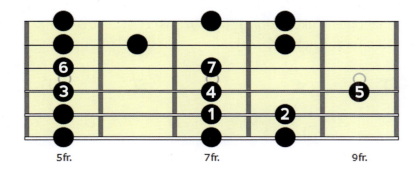

Here in E Phrygian the chord tones (1, 3, and 5) are landing on E, G and B. All the other notes are the passing notes for Phrygian. Make sense?

If it hasn't all clicked for you just yet, the more you work with it the better your brain understands it. There will literally be a "Lightbulb Moment", you'll feel it if you haven't already.

In this example of Phrygian, the numbers on the diagram no longer represent the 7 modes, the numbers are showing the "scale" of E phrygian.

This will help you with exactly what notes you should be targeting.

Your ear is very, very good at picking out what notes are target notes and what notes are passing notes, and that's just because you've been listening to music your whole life. Your ear is trained subconsciously for what notes fit and what notes don't.

This is something you need to be practicing over and over again. You want to really work on the sound of the chord tones for each mode. We're gonna dive into the target notes for each mode a bit more in the next chapter.

If the idea of focusing on certain notes while you are improvising feels overwhelming to you right now, that's OK, just leave it for now and come back to it when you feel more comfortable with it all. We have really gone through a lot of information, you need to take your time to digest it all, and the time for that is different for each person. You will know yourself, when you are ready to get into this.

And remember… The scale patterns have done the hard work for us, even if you don't focus 'intentionally' on these notes, you'll likely end up doing it accidentally because they just so happen to sound the best!

What Chords Are In A Key?

One of the biggest bonuses to learning all of the information you have learned so far, is you now have a super easy way of figuring out all of the chords you can play in a key. We simply use the information we've memorized from the modes. Take a look at this familiar chart showing the major scale formula, the note numbers, and the notes for the key of C Major.

T	T	s	T	T	T	s
1	2	3	4	5	6	7
C	D	E	F	G	A	B

All we need to do to find out the chords for the key is add the information we already know about the modes to the correct number.

1. Ionian - (Natural) **Major**
2. Dorian - **minor**
3. Phrygian - **minor**
4. Lydian - **Major**
5. Mixolydian - **Major**
6. Aeolian - (Natural) **minor**
7. Locrian - **diminished**

Since numbers 1, 4 & 5 are Major, we play Major chords for those notes. Numbers 2, 3 & 6 are minor, so we add the lower case 'm' onto the note name (as you can see below) to represent the fact that they are minor chords. And number 7 is diminished (we'll talk more about diminished chords later when we get into triads).

	T	T	s	T	T	T	s
	1	2	3	4	5	6	7
	C	Dm	Em	F	G	Am	Bdim

Write out the notes (and chords) for a few random keys using the "fill in the blanks" guide below:

	T	T	s	T	T	T	s
	1	2m	3m	4	5	6m	7dim

	T	T	s	T	T	T	s
	1	2m	3m	4	5	6m	7dim

	T	T	s	T	T	T	s
	1	2m	3m	4	5	6m	7dim

	T	T	s	T	T	T	s
	1	2m	3m	4	5	6m	7dim

As you continue through The GPR System™, more and more of the information should be sinking in.

If for any reason you get 'stuck', take a break. You'll want to review the chapters of this book often, especially from Chapter #4 all the way through to the end. You'll see everything from a new perspective the second time through. Take as much time as you need for this to all sink in.

And if you have the optional video program to go along with this book, watch through those videos to reinforce what we have covered here and to see more examples.

If you haven't experienced the Lightbulb moments, trust in the process, they're guaranteed to come your way the more you review the information!

Moving The Modes To Different Keys

We're gonna keep it simple and continue using the G Diatonic scale pattern.

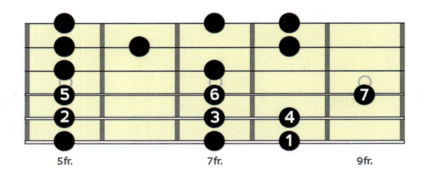

Step #1: Choose a mode (Represented by a number).

Step #2: Choose a key/note (For instance "E").

Step #3: Move the number of the mode you want onto the note you want.

For instance, if you wanted to play E Mixolydian you'd take the number 5 on the "D" string and move it so that it lands on an "E" note. Doing so positions the 'G diatonic scale pattern' and all the others that link together to it, into the key of E Mixolydian.

If you wanted to play D Lydian, simply grab the Lydian root note (#4) and position the scale pattern so that it lands on a "D" note on that string (in this instance, the 5th fret of the "A" string).

F Dorian? Just grab the Dorian root note and place it onto the 8th fret so that it's landing on an "F" note.

I go through a bunch of examples for moving the modes into different keys in the optional video course, so if you have that, go and refer to that to see examples on the fretboard.

You can use this exact system for any of the other diatonic scale patterns, but it's always good to have one you really rely on, and the 'G Pattern' has been our anchor the whole time... Whether it's for the Pentatonic patterns, Blues scales, Full major scales or the Modes.

Each mode has its own "mood", and you need to spend some time playing each of them to really learn the characteristics of each of them. That's where the "Drone Jam Track" you have is perfect for this. This track is just one constant note, which means you can play ANY mode over it.

For instance, if it's a A Drone Jam Track, then you can play A Ionian, A Dorian, A Phrygian, A Lydian, A Mixolydian, A Aeolian and A Locrian all over the same track by position the scales to be in the right mode.

Using The Single Chord Backing Tracks With Different Modes

Remember, modes are determined by the backing music you are playing over. I've given you some single chord backing tracks to really help you dial in on each mode. Because the single chord backing tracks never change to different chords, it leaves them open for us to play different modes over them.

The one thing we have to keep in mind is that if the track is played with a major chord you MUST use a major mode, and if the track is played with a minor chord you MUST use a minor mode. Use the single chord jam/backing tracks and experiment playing different modes over them.

REMEMBER: Out in the real world, you cannot decide to change the mode of a backing track, we can only do this because these tracks are played with 1 single chord that repeats over and over again.

What Modes Can I Play to Each Track?

C Ionian track is played with a C major chord, so you can play either C Ionian, C Lydian, or C Mixolydian

D Dorian track is played with a D minor chord, so you can play either D Dorian, D Phrygian, or D Aeolian

E Phrygian is played with an E minor chord, so you can either play E Dorian, E Phrygian, or E Aeolian.

F Lydian is played with an F major chord so you can either play F Ionian, F Lydian, or F Mixolydian.

G Mixolydian is played with a G major chord, so you can either play G Ionian, G Lydian, G Mixolydian.

A Aeolian is played with an A minor chord, so you can play A dorian, A phrygian, or A Aeolian.

NOTE: Locrian is diminished so it can't be swapped around like the others, and diminished chords are never (usually) held onto for very long, so no jam track is supplied for this.

Mode Flavors

Each of the modes has their own "Flavor" which can take some time to really feel. However, use the list below to give you some ideas on what the mode flavors *"lean"* towards...

Ionian - *Natural Major*

Dorian - *Blues Minor*

Phrygian - *Spanish Minor*

Lydian - *Jazz Major*

Mixolydian - *Blues Major*

Aeolian - *Natural Minor*

Locrian - *Diminished*

There are a huge amount of songs you will know in all modes (except Locrian, but people have still written using this mode).

I recommend going to Google or YouTube right now and searching for "Song in (insert mode here)" and have a listen through. You'll find some songs you know already, see how they make you feel and start to associate those songs & feelings with the modes they are created in.

You can also try playing modes over modes...this doesn't always sound good and takes some practice, but it does work.

Here's what I mean: If you're playing in A Aeolian, instead of emphasizing the "A" note try emphasizing the "E" note (which would be phrygian). Because this isn't the "Natural Mode" of the backing music, you REALLY have to sell the "E" note for this to work.

Another trick that'll help you move around the fretboard with ease is identifying 2 string blocks. Which we will dive into on the next page...

2 String Blocks

These will help you move around the fretboard between patterns because they are the same notes per 2 strings, just in different octaves.

For instance, in the example below, you have the entire fretboard linked up in using the Diatonic scale patterns in the key of C Major (or A minor, or any mode you want it to be!).

Look at the highlighted notes, 6 notes that are really easy to see. The next diagram shows the same pattern, 2 frets higher, on the next 2 strings. And again 3 frets higher on the highest 2 strings. The fretboard is full of these patterns that you can use to "hack" your way from one end of the fretboard to the other.

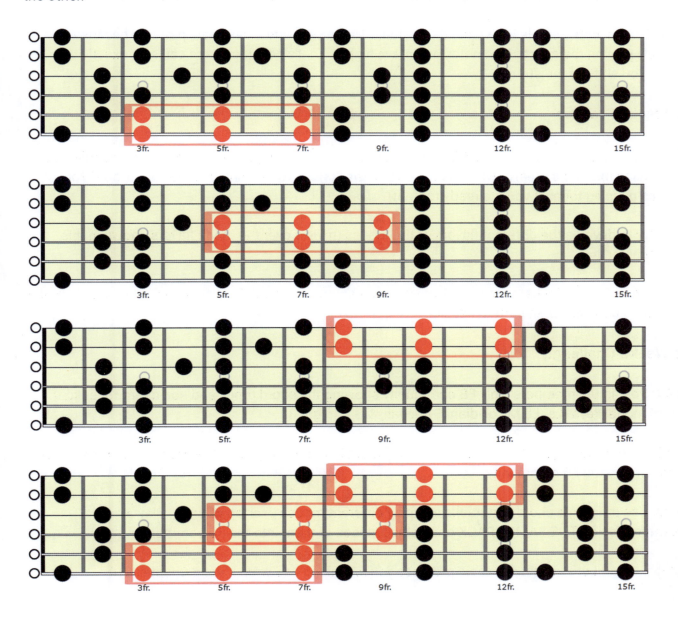

Try this example out yourself. This works for ANY 2 string block. What I mean is... Grab any notes that work together on the low E and A strings, and you will be able to use the following system to move up the fretboard using only that pattern.

2 String Blocks System

1. Identify a 2 string block (this is ANY combination notes that work together on the low E and A strings).

2. Move up to the D & G strings, and shift over 2 frets. The notes will be there too.

3. Finally, move up to the B & high E strings and shift over 3 frets. The notes are here also.

2 String Blocks work seamlessly within the Diatonic, Pentatonic and blues scale patterns because you are simply playing the exact same notes an octave higher. That's how the shape can stay exactly the same as you shift up the strings.

This Week's Practice

1. Practice soloing in all of the different modes along to the supplied backing tracks (found in your online members area/downloads). Focus on the "Chord Tones" and use the "Non-Chord Tones" as passing tones if you are ready for that.

2. Try to develop the different flavors of the modes (review over the mode flavors shown in this chapter).

3. Use "2 String Blocks" to move effortlessly across the fretboard. Find as many as you can to make transitions between patterns easier.

This Week's Challenge

Part #1: Post in the members' only FB community showing the chord tones and non-chord tones to the 3 different modal keys (I.e. Eb Mixolydian, F Aeolian, & G Phrygian).

Part #2: Fill out the page in this chapter with 4 different keys showing all of the chords that are available and post it into the FB community.

Part #3: Use the single chord jam tracks and play different modes overtop of them. Play at least 2 different modes on THE SAME TRACK and upload videos of them into the FB community.

Great job so far! Let's keep up the epic progress you're making and wrap it up in Chapter #10.

CHAPTER #10

You've made it, and there's one final lesson here that's really going to keep you moving forward and growing as a guitar player as much as humanly possible…

Simplifying The Modes

If you're having trouble keeping the modes: "simple".. Answer these two questions…

Do you know how to improvise in the key of A minor using the Diatonic scale?

Do you know how to improvise in the key of C major using the Diatonic scale?

If you answered "Yes" to both of those questions, you're already playing the modes. Remember, as soon as we use the diatonic scales, that…

Major = Natural Major = Ionian.

And Minor = Natural Minor = Aeolian.

So you already knew 2 of the modes before you learned the other 5. It's easy to let our minds complicate the modes because of the fancy names they've been given, but remember that the names just link to a number, 1 - 7.

The modes will become a lot clearer to you by following through with my recommendations you'll find later on in the chapter. Now, just before we change topic, I want to remind you of this…

> *"Your eyes can't see something that's right in front of you when they're focused on the mountains in the distance"*

If you ever feel the modes are becoming complicated in your mind, sit back, review these chapters and constantly ask this question…

"Where is the simplicity?"

Because when you seek, you will find.

And one more time… You already knew 2 of the modes before you learned about the other 5, so you're already playing 2 of the modes whether you like it or not!

Playing To The Chords

We've covered focusing on the "Target Notes" for the key we are in. We've covered focusing on the "Chord Tones" and using the "Non-Chord Tones" as passing notes…

Now we're going to take it one step further. THIS is what will help you hit those magic notes, every single time.

There are 2 levels to this…

LEVEL #1: Focus on the *"Root Note"* of each chord.

LEVEL #2: Focus on the *"Chord Tones"* of each chord.

Each Chord? What does that mean?

It means that every time the backing music you're soloing over changes to a different chord, you focus on different notes on the fretboard (Inside of the scale patterns you already know).

This applies for all of the scale types you've learned. Pentatonic, Blues, and Diatonic (Including all of the modes).

One of the jam tracks I've given you is titled "Play To The Chords Jam Track". This is in the key of A minor and uses the chords Am, Dm and Em. You won't have any visual cues as to what chord is being played when, as you don't ever get those when playing along to any other track.

This will take some time, just take it piece by piece. First start out by playing the root notes ONLY as the chords move throughout the jam track, then as you start getting comfortable with that, add a few more notes in.

Before too long, you'll really start to understand how to use this concept and the power of it.

This is really something you need to spend the time doing, you can't just understand it then expect your hands to follow suit, it takes a bit of practice.

You'll be targeting the notes for the chords A minor, D minor and E Minor.

Head over to your members area and play through the "Playing To The Chords" backing track if you haven't already.

Right now I'm going to show you another little "hack" to find the chord tones for level #2 of playing to the chords. Which is to use major and minor triads to quickly and easily find the "Chord Tones" of a chord. You'll also find the diminished triad below, you won't use it very much but it's important to know.

Chord Triads

What is a "Chord Triad"?

A chord triad is the 3 notes that make up that chord. You need 3 notes to make the most common chords in music (Major & minor). They are the root, the 5th and the 3rd (Major or minor 3rd).

The only difference between a Major chord and a minor chord is the 3rd is either a Major 3rd, or a minor 3rd. They are only one fret apart as you'll see in the following diagrams.
Here's 3 simple shapes to find the notes for any Major, minor or diminished triads.

- If a chord is a **MAJOR** chord, then use a MAJOR triad to find the chord tones.

- If a chord is a **MINOR** chord, then use a MINOR triad to find the chord tones

- If the chord is a **DIMINISHED** chord, then use a DIMINISHED triad to find the chord tones.

You might be asking yourself...

"If it only takes 3 notes to play a chord, why do most of the chords I play have more than 3 notes?"

For any Major or minor chord, you are actually only playing 3 notes, those 3 notes can be played in any order (as long as the lowest note is the root note) over and over again in different octaves.

E.g. The standard open E minor chord you know has three "E" notes, two "B" notes and one "G" note.

Triads are the building blocks of chords. And luckily, as you'll see on the next page, the shapes of them are very easy to remember.

These shapes will allow you to find the notes of any Major, minor or diminished chord. Simply put the root note of the triad onto the note of the chord you want and then use your knowledge of how to name every note on the fretboard to figure out what notes are in the triad/chord.

NOTE: These triad shapes work when the root note is on the Low E string or the A string

 = Major Root Note

Major Triad

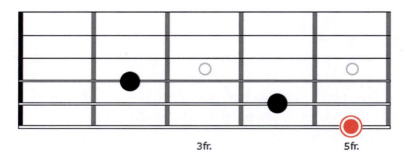

Minor Triad

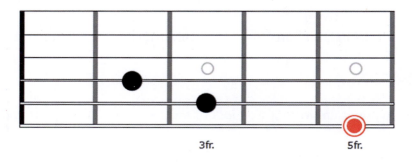

Diminished Triad

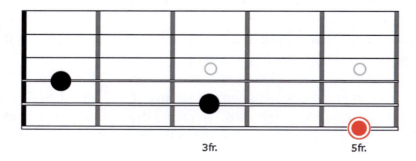

You might find that when you are improvising that you have been using these "chord tones" as notes you play more, or hang on intuitively. If so, that's likely because you have been subconsciously training your ear for all these years listening to your favorite songs.

Finding The Taste - What Scales To Use?

You know A LOT of different ways to use the fretboard now…So what scale or mode should you use?

It's different for each situation, sometimes it will be dictated to you by the kind of music (AKA, it makes sense to use the Blues scales over Blues music) and other times, it can be completely your choice. The scale patterns you can choose from are…

- Pentatonic
- Blues
- Diatonic (including the modes)
- Or a mixture of all of the above

You are the decision-maker for each situation, and that comes from experience. Good news is you can switch between them very, very easily. Remember that you can always strip things back to the Pentatonic scale patterns and add in notes from there to create the other scales.

You have 2 "drone" tracks using an "A" note in your jam tracks section. One version that has some drums playing along to give you a beat, and another with just the drone itself, so you can forget about timing and really focus on the notes themselves.

These drone tracks are great to practice mixing everything up as the drone tracks don't *"discriminate against"* or *"dictate"* what type of scale you use.

This means anything will sound good as long as you're in a key that uses "A" as it's tonic (home note). You can play A Major or minor Pentatonic, A Major or minor Blues, and ANY mode in the key of A.

If you're playing in a Major or minor key (AKA. A mode that is natural major, or natural minor) follow these simple steps to guarantee you find the right scale to use…

1. Start with the pentatonic scale - this is our skeleton. Everything else we can think of is just adding extra notes.

2. Add in some blues notes. Does it sound good? If so, keep 'em, if not, throw them out.

3. Add in some Diatonic notes. Does it sound good? If so, keep 'em, if not, throw them out.

It comes down to your ears…if it sounds good, keep doing it!

The best guitar players in the world mash in between all the scale types all time. Once you have these down, you want to blur the lines between Pentatonic, Blues and Diatonic while still having the ability to play strictly one of them when it comes time to do so.

I first learned this after learning some of Jimmy Page's solos. The way he walks in and out of different scale pattern types is fantastic, and really showed me that all of these scale pattern types are tools and you pull on them when you need them.

My personal favorite is to play a mix of all of them. I like my solos to have a bluesy feel, even when the song isn't necessarily bluesy. When you're writing your own music, you make the rules.

A Visual Concept Of What You've Learned

There's plenty of ways to look at the information you've learned. And the building block approach you've been learning is called the Guitar Pattern Recognition System™ (GPR System™).

Looking back, everything will make sense. You now have the knowledge to watch any guitar player, and if you look close enough, be able to tell what patterns they are using. INSTANTLY understanding so much more about what that guitar player is doing. Whether you're watching a band play in your local town, or watching a live concert of your favorite band on TV, your mind can now recognize patterns that guitar players are using for their solos & lead playing.

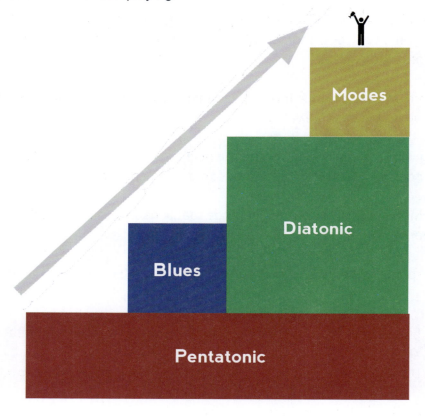

You built your fretboard foundation for 4 solid weeks. You then added a block to create the blues scales. You added diatonic notes to build things further. Then the modes pretty much fell into place for you, because all you had to do was build from your original Fretboard Skeleton.

You Now Know...

- The 5 pentatonic patterns that link up the entire fretboard into a complete "grid"
- The root notes (Major & minor) for each pattern
- How the patterns are built from the open chord shapes they are named after
- How to position the pentatonic patterns to be in a major or minor key
- How to improvise
- How to transpose (move) a solo into a different key
- How to write your own guitar solos
- Target notes to focus on for each key
- How to play the blues note
- Full Major Scale theory
- The 5 Diatonic scale patterns & How they link up over the fretboard
- What notes inside of the patterns you can bend, and where to bend to
- The 7 Mode names and if they are Major, minor or diminished
- How to play a pentatonic scale in any key
- How to play diatonic scale in any key
- How to play all of the modes
- How to focus on chord tones and use non-chord tones as passing notes
- What chords are in any key
- Plus much more...

I tried out 5 different online companies and found out that there were gaps in the way they taught guitar. They either assumed you knew everything they were talking about or simply told you that you should already know something. I had no idea what they were talking about. Or they use their class as a platform to show off their own skills.

Charlie teaches differently. He wants you to ask questions. He monitors your progress. And most importantly, he really cares about teaching you guitar. ***I wish this stuff was available 20 or 30 years ago.***

- **Ken May**, *California, USA*

Integrating Back Into Society

The title of this page is a bit tongue and cheek…However, there are some important factors here you need to understand… You now harness immense knowledge of the fretboard, but it is by no means "complete". There's ALWAYS more to learn, more to discover. It's all part of the adventure.

Keep in mind, some people have learned how to do things in different ways so if you speak to another guitar player and you mention the "G Pentatonic pattern" they might say… "NO! This is called Box #1!"…

And if that's how they've learned it, that's cool. I'd recommend not interfering unless you're happy to walk them through EVERYTHING you've learned in this book… Because there's a lot to it. Keep this in mind… You know more than 99% of guitar players will EVER know.

"There's more than one road to the airport", you just took the GPR System™ highway

With great power comes great responsibility (as a very famous superhero comic once quoted). Use this information you've gained to enjoy playing guitar, and also to share your playing with your friends, family, and future fans. You have held the key, you've twisted the lock, you've taken a giant leap through the door…   …The rest is now up to you.

This Week's Practice

1. Practice playing the different modes to the A drone tracks (found in your downloads) these will help you grasp the modes even further.

2. Practice playing to the chords with the supplied track in A minor. Use level #1, focusing on the root note of each chord to begin with (Am, Dm, and Em) then move to Level #2 (focusing on the chord tones).

3. Memorize the Major, Minor and Diminished triads.

This Week's Challenges

Part #1: Record a video of you improvising to either the A drone track with rhythm or the A drone track (without rhythm) mixing between pentatonic, blues and diatonic scale and upload it into the members community.

Part #2: Record a video of you "playing to the chords" to the supplied jam track in A minor, even if it's just the root notes, and upload it to the members community.

That wraps up The GPR System™! Congratulations!

Want A Deeper Understanding? Want To Become A Better Guitar Player?

Head back to Chapter #4 and continue through Chapters 5, 6, 7, 8, 9, and 10 again. The second time through, you'll discover more and further cement your knowledge of everything into your mind. Most people aren't willing to do what it takes to become the guitar player they've always dreamed of being… don't be one of those people!

Commit to reviewing the GPR System™ from Chapter #4, the results will speak for themselves and many members who have done this have been blown away by the improvements they made simply by reviewing this information again.

If when you go back to Chapter #4 some things still seem a bit hazy, go back from week #1…

I promise, you'll be VERY glad you did.

"Most people think they're going to listen or read something one time and change, But the problem is that the subconscious mind doesn't work that way, there are so many things competing for the attention of your subconscious mind. It's only when you listen or read something over and over that it manages to cut through the noise and your subconscious realizes "this is important."

Go through this workshop a second time (maybe even more) and you'll discover just how much you missed the first time through. You'll discover "*hidden gems*" that'll help make you the great guitar player you know you can be.

From one musician to another… Thank you for letting me share the GPR System™ with you, it has changed my life and I know it can change yours.

Congratulations on your amazing effort.

To your guitar playing success!

Charlie Wallace
Guitar Mastery Method

BONUS CHAPTER

Mixing Major & Minor Pentatonic (Aka: The 'Hybrid' Scale)

Note: You MUST have a very strong understanding of the pentatonic scale patterns and how they all link together, as well as the blues notes. Or else this lesson will not make any sense. Review over the previous weeks of the workshop if you need to.

We mix Major & minor together to create a very Bluesy sound. BUT, there are some important factors we need to take into consideration.

We can only mix Major and minor when we are playing STANDARD Blues, not 'Minor' Blues. Remember how with Blues music we are (usually) playing minor scales over a Major backing? That's why this works, the backing is already in a Major key.

If the blues track you are playing over specifically says 'Minor Blues', it will probably be best to stick to minor pentatonic/blues scale patterns.

How To Use The Major Notes

You'll notice in the diagrams on the next page that the entire fretboard is shown with the scale patterns linked up in the key of A minor (by now, you should be able to discern between the patterns without them being labeled). The Blues notes are there, as well as the Major notes which are shown as red hollow circles.

Use the Major notes the same way you would a blues note, they're not the best notes to hang onto, but sound great as passing notes. If you want to see a master use the hybrid scale, just go watch Stevie Ray Vaughan.

In the optional video course, I give some examples of how to use these Major notes, so if you have that, I highly recommend you go watch through this bonus chapters video now.

I don't recommend that you practice this hybrid scale as you have practiced all of the previous patterns you have learned, as this is a mash up of more than one pattern. What I recommend is that you use the 80/20 approach shown in the 2nd diagram (80/20 meaning you can get 80% of the benefit by using only 20% of the extra notes).

Jam along to a Blues jam track in the key of A with these diagrams in front of you and start experimenting using the Major notes as passing notes. Hammer on and pull straight back off, use one of the notes as you walk up the scale, play one of the notes then quickly bend up to one of the regular pentatonic notes... There are so many fun ways to use them.

Blues Scales Linked Up With Added Major Notes

◯ = Added Major Note

◯ = Blues Note

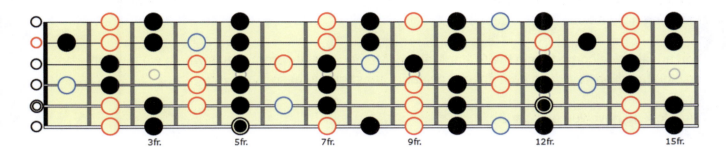

80/20 Approach (Get started Easily By Adding Major Notes To Your G+3 Anchor)

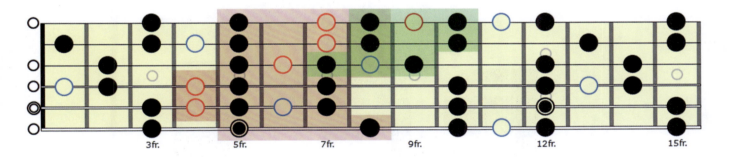

Where To From Here?...

If you've loved what you've learned so far and you want to further develop your guitar skills, grow your confidence, and have more fun on your guitar than ever before...

Become a member of Guitar Mastery Method TODAY.

Get started with a FREE trial. Just visit **www.GuitarMasteryMethod.com/FREE** and create your membership with us.

You are also welcome to join the Guitar Mastery Method social communities where we run contests, do epic guitar giveaways, and host special celebrity guest guitar lessons for you.

We'd love to have you on board!

I'll see you in there.

- Charlie Wallace

P.S. If you're one of those strange humans that skips to the back of the book before you finish... shame on you 😛 But then again... maybe you're like me - You just want the ultimate fast track to playing your favorite songs, like your favorite guitarists... And you likely want the confidence that comes with it so you can instantly impress friends, family, and future fans with the whip crack of your guitar pick, right? So maybe what I've shared with all the awesome individuals who have already completed the book and are experiencing these kinds of things already interests you too... If so - Get all the guitar hacks and shortcuts & become a member today by visiting this link right here: **www.GuitarMasteryMethod.com/FREE**